DATE DUE

**Check for CD in
back pocket.**

SEP - - 2001

SIMON ESTES:
IN HIS OWN VOICE

AN AUTOBIOGRAPHY

SIMON ESTES

AND MARY L. SWANSON

SIMON ESTES: IN HIS OWN VOICE
Copyright © 1999 Simon Estes

Published by LMP, L.C.
A Landauer Company
12251 Maffitt Road, Cumming, Iowa 50061

President: Jeramy Lanigan Landauer
Vice President: Becky Johnston
Managing Editor: Marlene Hemberger Heuertz
Art Director: Robert Mickey Hager
Editor: Linda Delbridge, Ph.D.
Associate Editor: Sarah Reid
Contributing Editors: Marjon Schaefer and Wayne T. Messerly
Cover Design: Laurel Albright
Graphics Technician: Stewart Cott
Photographers: Craig Anderson and Dennis Kennedy

This book is printed on acid-free paper.
Printed in Hong Kong

Library of Congress Catalog Card Number: 98-075760

ISBN Number: 1-890621-01-3 h/c
ISBN Number: 1-890621-03-X s/c

10 9 8 7 6 5 4 3 2 1

DEDICATION

FROM SIMON ESTES

To

my daughters, Jennifer,

Lynne, and Tiffany

and my mother

Ruth Estes

whom I love with all my heart

FOREWORD

Since 1996, we have heard often-harrowing stories about gross human rights violations in South Africa as members of that country's Truth and Reconciliation Commission.

As I read Simon Estes' story, it was as if I was listening to the same kind of testimony that has come before our Commission. Some of what he recounts is truly heart-rending, such as the account of how his father died of a ruptured appendix and being accosted by an unfeeling and arrogant physician. It seemed to be a death that could have been prevented had the patient been white; or when the mortgage on their home was foreclosed after his father's death. It has all sounded so familiar—police suspecting that the new Mercedes Benz that he was driving could only have been stolen.

It could all have happened in the old apartheid South Africa. One has constantly been amazed in the Commission at the pettiness and also the awfulness of the evil of racism.

But more wonderfully, one has been overwhelmed by the magnanimity, the nobility of spirit of those who having suffered so grievously were yet ready to forgive their tormentors.

I was deeply moved reading Simon Estes' story, and I have marvelled that despite all the anguish he has suffered, he could be so whole, so magnanimous, so ready to forgive and not to nurse grudges, that he could go on the stage despite all that pain and regale the world with such a magnificent voice.

Simon Estes is indeed a worthy role model!

The Most Rev. Desmond M. Tutu
Archbishop Emeritus of Cape Town
at the South African Consulate,
New York City, New York

In the title role of Simon Boccanegra

SIMON ESTES: IN HIS OWN VOICE

Introduction

"…rolling, voluminous sound" (*Time*)…."A powerful voice and a strong stage presence!" (*Chicago Tribune*)…."Sings with the highest degree of interpretation" (*Pravda*, Moscow)…."…an unusually talented singer" (*Christian Science Monitor*)…."He left the audience shouting in the aisles" (*Sunday Telegraph*, Sydney)…."…splendidly rich-voiced…." (*International Herald Tribune*)…."…voluminous and at the same time elegant…" (*Vienna Zeitung*)…."…displayed deep emotion and musical mastery…great talent and an extraordinary voice" (*Morgenpost*, Berlin)…."imposing…noble, musical, aware…even haunting" (*Boston Globe*)…."With the singer-actor Simon Estes, a star was born. He is superior to all his predecessors in the role [of the Dutchman]" (*Nachrichten*, Nuremburg)…. "Here the nobility of expression must be at its highest point." (*Tagesspiegel*, Berlin)

The Washington Opera
OPERA HOUSE

Simon Boccanegra

Fri Nov 13, 1998
8:00 PM

Simon Estes

Account Number
423395

BOX SEAT
19   3

COMP $.00

$239.00
No Refunds

Thank you for joining us at the Opera

Mr. Simon Estes

How far he has come, this son of a coal miner and grandson of a slave! How much he has accomplished! He glances at the image in the mirror as make-up artists transform him from Simon Estes the man to Simon Estes as Simon Boccanegra, his 100th role during his 35-year career. He thoughtfully insists "blessed" best describes his life and career.

His poor, humble childhood years were richly blessed with faith and love, determination and persistence, patience and forgiveness modeled by strong parents. At the age of eight, Simon began singing in church with his family. During his university days, his mentor introduced Simon to classical music and encouraged the development of his exceptional ability.

After a year at The Juilliard School of Music, Simon made his debut in 1965 with the Deutsche Oper Berlin as Ramfis in *Aida*. 1966 brought third place in the Tchaikovsky Competition and a White House appearance. His major breakthrough occurred when he sang the title role in *The Flying Dutchman* in Zurich in 1976.

This internationally renowned bass-baritone is best known as King Philip in *Don Carlo*, Escamillo in *Carmen*, Wotan in Wagner's *Ring Cycle*, Amfortas in *Parsifal*, Porgy in *Porgy and Bess*, his four roles in *The Tales of Hoffmann*, and the title roles of Boris Godunov, the Flying Dutchman, and Macbeth. In demand as a soloist and recitalist, Simon has performed with the world's most prominent orchestras and conductors in its finest opera houses and recital halls. He has sung for five United States presidents and numerous other world leaders. He has recorded on more than ten labels.

From the pain of prejudice experienced as a young child to the frustration of being bypassed as an accomplished performer, the racial discrimination Simon has known and his peaceful but persistent response are as integral to this man as fire to refining gold.

As Simon shares both his voice and his determination to make a difference in the world, his music becomes a means for his message. Because of his own struggles as an impoverished college student attending classes and working full-time to support his mother, his brother, and himself, Simon Estes has established

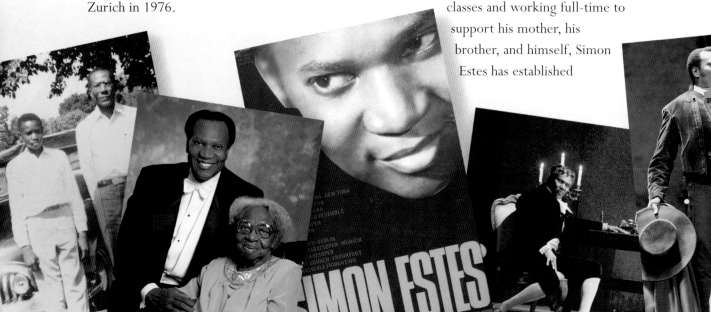

several scholarship programs for talented students who otherwise could not afford college. As witness to his success, he has been invited to participate in peace conferences, students and faculty named a South African high school in his honor, and he remains a tireless advocate for talented young African-American artists.

The student has become the mentor. Simon eagerly talks with young people, sharing with them the importance of peace, the need for solid values, and the role of determination in achieving goals. He conducts master classes for gifted young singers. He gets them to the right schools, the right people, and the right experiences so they can develop their gifts and share them with the world.

Simon Estes—the goodwill ambassador—has been honored by small towns and nations, by citizen groups and international leaders who recognize his extraordinary commitment to people and institutions. His foundation targets health and educational needs of children around the world. He prays daily that God will continue to give him courage and strength so he can help others.

Moments before he will walk on stage as Simon Boccanegra, Simon Estes prays quietly. "Dear God, thank you for the gift to sing, the gift to love, the gift to share, the gift to care."

Few in the waiting audience would know that even though the physical Simon Estes appearance is being changed to that of the character he is about to portray, he is still aware of who he is and from where he has come. How did a skinny little boy from Centerville, Iowa, who thought he would never get farther east than Chicago make it *here*?

And the answer, a story of how faith and integrity triumph over adversity and discrimination, is best told by Simon Estes himself…in his own voice.

— *Linda Delbridge, Ph. D., Editor*

In the role of King Philip, from "Don Carlo"

CONTENTS

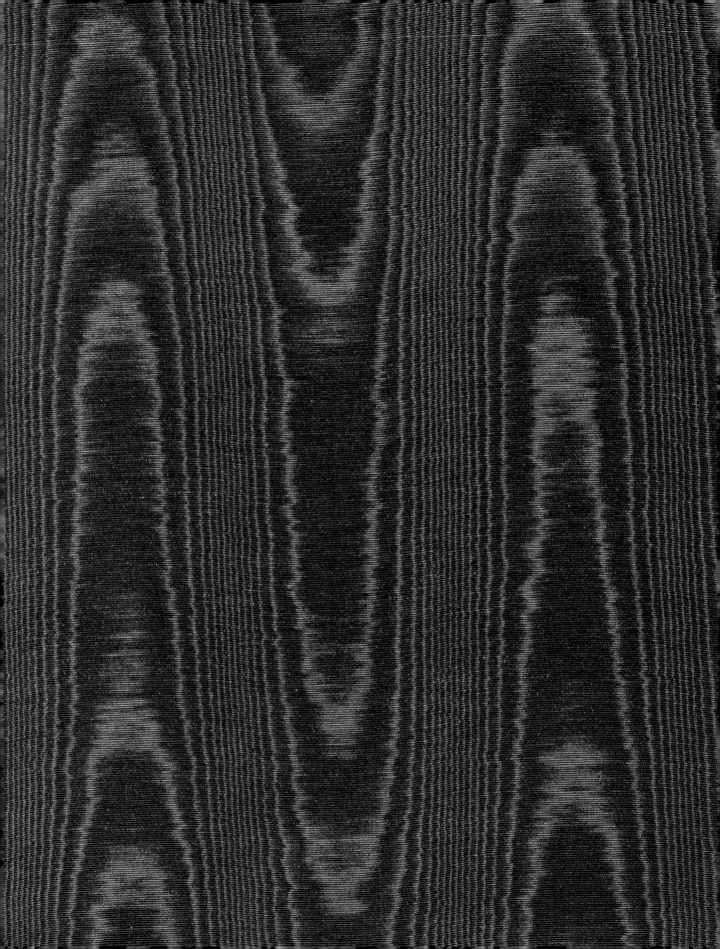

CHAPTER ONE

The Man

My career has carried me into exclusive enclaves of society where people ask, "Who is the most important person you have ever met?" My answer always surprises them. Although I've sung for popes, presidents, royalty, and some of the world's most recognized celebrities, the most important person who ever sat in any audience was my mother, followed closely by my daughters, sisters, and brother. My deepest regret is that my father's untimely death prevented his hearing me sing professionally.

My parents provided the strong foundation on which I have built my life: bricks and mortar made of faith, sound morals, honesty, courage, and stamina. Without my parents' love and support, nothing I have accomplished would have been possible.

My father's heritage was both Native American and African-American. His grandfather was a Native American, and his parents were slaves. At the age of five, my father's father was sold for $500 (shortly before President Lincoln signed the Emancipation Proclamation in 1863). Because he was quite large for his age, he brought a higher price of $100 for each year of his life.

The Hutchinson family who bought my grandfather moved from Virginia to Missouri, where my grandfather worked on their farm and later began his own family. The Hutchinsons gave my grandparents land to farm and a house for their family. They were good, generous people. White people respected my grandfather, "Major Estes," and seldom started prayer meetings without him.

My grandparents raised twelve children—nine boys and three girls. One of their sons, born in 1891, was my father, Simon Estes, which makes me only the third generation away from slavery.

My father's parents

Father

During my father's childhood, education was not considered important for blacks. As soon as a child was a good size and appeared strong enough for physical labor, he or she left school to tend the cattle or work in the fields. For a few years, my father attended a "colored" school.

Like most of the schools set aside for blacks, the facilities were minimal and the learning materials outdated, worn, and scarce. As soon as he finished the third grade, my father left school to work in the fields. As a result, he never had the opportunity to learn to read or write. After he met my mother, she taught him to write his name and read a little, which was the extent of his education.

After serving in World War I, my father visited his brother Oakey in Centerville, Iowa, and decided to stay. In the early 1900s, the soil in south central Iowa was rich with "black dia-monds"— bituminous coal. My father signed on as a coal miner, working long 12- to 14-hour days in the dark, damp earth. Because the coal veins were only 30"–40" thick, my father, like the other miners, had to lie on his side, day after day, using a large pick axe to break up the coal.

While black was the color of treasure below ground, it was not favored above ground when it involved black humans. Centerville was typical of any place in the United States in its attitude about the "colored" or the "foreign." It was acceptable to work, raise a family, and worship at a church of our choice provided we stayed within our social strata.

During his time in Centerville, my father became acquainted with Nathaniel Jeter, a coal miner and one of the first black delegates to a national union convention. Mr. Jeter's lovely daughter Ruth caught my father's eye. He courted her and, despite the nineteen-year age difference, they fell in love and married. Mother always says she could not have found a better husband for her or a better father for her children than Simon Estes.

Bouts of asthma aggravated by the dampness of the mines shortened my father's years as a coal miner. He then worked at a variety of jobs. He washed cars at local dealerships, fired furnaces during the winter, carted luggage at the Continental Hotel, and cleaned a movie theater.

I have been told that in 1940, Iowa's popula-tion contained only 0.7% "negro" people. When I was growing up in Centerville, blacks performed menial jobs. My father's earnings never totaled more than $40 a week, with the average usually only $20–25. How my parents managed to raise five children on his wages is beyond me.

My father's Native American heritage surfaced in his deportment and carriage. As a very stoic man, he embodied the extraordinary attributes of his ancestry.

My father fell in love with the daughter of Nathaniel Jeter, who is pictured here in the back row with those attending a national union convention.

Our house didn't have running water or indoor plumbing until I was 14. My father began his day before 6:00 AM, came home from his job after 7:00 PM, had a bite to eat, and dug a water line to our house until after 10:00 PM. When darkness interfered, he placed a coal oil lamp on the edge of the trench so he could work those extra hours.

My father dug the ditch a half block, from Jackson Street down to our house on 21st Street. I can't remember if he actually laid the pipe, but due to our financial situation, I'm positive he provided most of the labor. When the last pipe was laid, it was a day to celebrate. Finally, my family had running water and a toilet right inside the house. The outhouse was history!

The only source of fuel for the potbelly stove in our living room was scrap coal that fell off the trucks at the mines. When coal was unavailable, we burned cardboard or wooden boxes. Unlike rich people, we slept soundly on long, freezing winter nights with no worries about the pilot light going out.

Later, my father bought an oil-burning stove, but despite this upgrade, we did not keep much warmer. Daddy cut holes in the downstairs ceiling so the heat would rise, but it was still very cold. If sleeping in a cold room is good for the body, we were one of the healthiest families in town.

Sometimes our family didn't have enough to eat. What we did have that money could not buy was a tremendous amount of love for God, love for each other, and respect for people's rights. We were very, very happy.

As a bellman at the Continental Hotel, my father's best days for tips were Tuesday through Thursday when traveling salesmen came to town. As children, we knew if we needed school supplies we would have to wait until he had earned enough money carrying bags to pay for them. Sometimes when the hotel had fewer guests, he reluctantly asked for an advance so we could buy the things we needed most.

Despite his lack of formal education or any book knowledge, my father could do many things. If he had been educated, I'm certain he would have been more than a bellhop at the local hotel. For instance, despite his limited education, my father had an uncanny ability to deal with numbers. According to him, knowing the numbers 1–10 was enough to solve any problem. Unfortunately, I did not inherit those mathematical genes.

My father was also very kind, considerate, determined, and strong. I don't recall ever hearing anybody talk in a negative manner about him. I can still picture his appearance because his Native American heritage surfaced in his deportment and carriage. As a very stoic man, he embodied the extraordinary attributes of his ancestry. Neighborhood children were attracted to his calm nature and the time and attention he gave them.

My father never allowed anything to hold him back. He often contended with racism and bigotry

Working at the Big Five Coal Company, "Simon Estes No. 6" brought money home based on the amount of coal he dug that day.

in the workplace, but he put his heart and soul into his family and his home.

While the lack of money prevented him from buying many things, he found other ways of providing them. After long workdays, he came home and worked in his garden, or refurbished the house, or dug ditches so we could have running water—all for the betterment of his family. By his example, he blessed us children with confidence, courage, determination, and strength. He instilled in us a love of God and took us to church twice on Sundays and once on Wednesdays.

My father, who could not afford to buy us material items, gave us so much more in his caring actions. For instance, we never rode in a cold car, and we always had transportation of some kind, usually in a second- or third-hand car. Daddy went to work around 5:00 AM to fire furnaces in private homes, but on extremely cold days, he came home to drive us to school. Because the car didn't have an adequate heater, he found his own way to make the trip a bit warmer. He heated bricks in the oven, wrapped them in rags, and arranged them near our feet to keep us warm. This was possible, of course, because in Centerville you could drive anyplace in five minutes.

He and Mother taught me to be strong, not bitter. They told me that bitterness is a negative force and nothing good comes from it. As a little boy, I would sometimes go to them nearly in tears and ask why someone had called me a hurtful name or excluded me. They reminded me of Christ's sufferings and explained that suffering helps build character. They directed me to pray for those who couldn't see beyond skin color and to live in peace with everyone.

Throughout my youth, my parents consistently stressed the need to get an education. "Once you have an education, they can't take it away from you," my father explained. They saw education as the only way out of poverty and oppression. When I help students get a college education today, I am sharing what my parents instilled.

My father died on October 10, 1961, at the age of 70 under tragic and needless circumstances. He was hospitalized in Centerville, but his illness went undiagnosed.

Mother called me in Iowa City (where I was a University student) with the news that my father was quite ill and they both needed me. I quickly drove to a Des Moines hospital to which he had been transferred and went immediately to his bedside. My father was in tremendous pain; tears streamed down his cheeks.

"Son, I'm having terrible, terrible pains in my stomach. Please do something."

Initially, he was hospitalized for heart problems, although he had no prior history of heart

disease. I thought it strange that he had severe abdominal pains instead of chest pains, so I approached his doctor that evening. I introduced myself and asked if a cardiologist could examine my father. The doctor looked at me and scornfully replied, "A what?"

I repeated my request, thinking he hadn't heard me.

"Where did you learn that word?"

"At school," I replied. "I'm a student."

"And what's a cardiologist?" he asked with contempt.

In a calm voice not meant in any way to be condescending, I explained the derivation of the word "cardiologist." He was so incensed that I, a black man, knew a medical term. He informed me that he was a doctor of internal medicine, and since the heart is inside the body, he didn't need another doctor's advice. He then offered to withdraw from the case.

"No," I replied as calmly as I could, "I don't want you to withdraw. You have to understand that I love my father very much and he is in such great abdominal pain. He's crying to me for help. I just wondered if he had something else wrong with him."

Again he offered to withdraw. Once more I declined saying, "No, don't, because he must stay here. We don't have any money. I thought since my father is complaining of agonizing stomach pains, if a cardiologist examined my father and ruled out heart trouble, the stomach pains could be treated."

His patronizing reply was, "Well, we're doing everything we can for him and he's probably going to die anyway."

My father never allowed anything to hold him back.

Those were the doctor's exact words. Then he walked away.

The next night about 2:00 AM, Mother and my sisters Westella and Erdyne were with me at my father's bedside. His last words were: "Son, please look after the family, and especially her" (meaning Erdyne). I took his hand and vowed, "Oh, Daddy, I'll take care of you, too. Everything will be okay."

My father drew his last breath and was gone. An autopsy revealed that he had not died of heart trouble but of a ruptured appendix.

In 1961, no one should have been allowed to die from appendicitis. I think of the agonizing pain my father experienced and how he suffered.

More than one friend told me, "Simon, that would have caused me to hate that doctor. I would have sued."

I must say, honestly, that hate or a lawsuit never entered my mind. As I look back on it now, maybe I should have sued—not for the monetary gains, but to make others aware of the indifference that led to my father's death.

I realize my father was 70 years old and may not have lived many more years anyway, but he was strong and healthy despite his lifetime bouts of asthma and hay fever. I wish more than anything he could have lived long enough to see me sing in opera houses around the world. I wish he could have enjoyed and loved my daughters. Even more important, I would have had his companionship longer.

Mother was only 51 when my father died. He had been so beautiful and so kind to her! She never remarried, insisting that she already had been married to the best husband in the world.

After my father's death, I experienced one of the most painful episodes of my life. Although my father had willed our house in Centerville to Mother, neither she nor I could make the payments. I was working, going to college, and trying to support my mother and younger brother Dwane who was still at home.

That house was so important to my parents. My father's loving, back-breaking labor converted that house into a home. It would make me very sad to lose the place he valued so highly.

In desperation, I drove home from Iowa City to negotiate with the man who held the mortgage. I was willing to work any kind of deal so Mother could stay in the house.

However, nothing I said could sway him. We lost the house. Shortly after that, I moved Mother and Dwane from the house, yard, and all they had ever known to a dingy basement apartment in Iowa City. I slept on the bathroom floor so Mother and Dwane could have the beds. The house in Centerville was sold and later demolished.

After my father passed away, Mother gave me $600, my father's entire insurance policy. We both needed the money badly, but she wanted to help pay my tuition. Mother assured me that my father would have wanted the insurance money spent that way.

After my father's death, Mother never remarried, insisting that she had already been married to the best husband in the world.

I was in the Old Gold Singers at the University of Iowa, and a man who drove the bus for our group was friendly to us all. In one of our conversations, I mentioned that my father had died and my mother had given me money from my father's insurance policy. It meant that after struggling through hunger and hard times, the rest of the school year would go more easily.

One evening, this man called on the phone and in a serious tone said, "Simon, I need to talk to you."

I felt honored he had chosen me. He began to cry as he related how his wife was going to divorce him if he didn't pay his bills. Could I lend him the $600 I had inherited?

Of course he would pay me back. He gave me the exact time when this payback would occur; I loaned him the money.

As the weeks passed and my own need for the money increased, I asked him for repayment. His response was rude. I realized he had no intention of paying me back. To this day, I have never seen a penny of that money which could have made my school years easier. I often wonder how this "friend" could have done that when he knew the circumstances under which I existed.

One October many years later, I visited Centerville to give a benefit concert. After breakfast that day, I felt the need to drive to Oakland Cemetery on the east side of town. It was dark, rainy, and cold, but something told me to go out there.

When I arrived at my father's tombstone, I realized it was the anniversary of his death. As I prayed, I felt a warmth on my face. Startled because the weather was cloudy, I looked up to see the sun coming through a very small opening in the clouds. While I continued to experience this incredible warmth, I closed my eyes to finish the prayer before the warm sun disappeared.

When Mother and I drove back to Des Moines that night, I shared my experience at the cemetery. Her explanation capped the day: "It was God's presence and it was God's spirit speaking through your father's spirit. God loves you and your father loves you"

This marker stands over my father's grave as a tribute to his service to his country.

Mother

My mother, Ruth Jeter, grew up poor in Centerville. Her mother gave birth to ten children and died at a young age, leaving her father, "Papa," to raise the children by himself.

Mother dropped out of school in the eleventh grade to go south to sing in a choir at the Piney Woods School in Mississippi. However, she didn't stay away for very long because she missed her Papa and her brothers and sisters. Even though it meant the end of her career with the choir, Mother chose to be with her family.

My love for music comes from my mother, and hers from her father. Papa loved music and made sure his children were exposed to it.

Mother never had a day of formal training but was born with a beautiful voice—a gift from God. My sisters Westella and Erdyne developed strong soprano and alto voices, while my sister Patty and I were blessed with exceptional voices and unbelievable ranges like Mother's. Despite her lack of training, Mother's gift became obvious as she sang solos in our church and with a small group in Centerville. At home whenever Mother had some free time in the evenings, she loved to play our old piano and sing.

After I moved Mother and my brother to Des Moines from Iowa City, Mother sang in the choir, played the piano, and taught the children's choir at the Corinthian Baptist Church for 32 years. She still plays the piano "a little bit at home, just to comfort myself."

Her love of Jesus and her church have always been the most important elements in Mother's life. In talking about today's church problems and conflicts, Mother says, "Don't let that keep you from going to church, because God is church. You just go and seek Him out and don't worry about those people."

Mother always tells me to put my trust in the Lord. "Jesus will be your best friend. People will disappoint you just as family members might, but He will never let you down. Make sure you put Him first."

Mother lives what is important in life: good character, honesty, and respect for others. She believes God teaches us to obey His laws and love our neighbors.

People often ask me, "Why don't you hate people who have mistreated you?" My mother is the reason. She taught me to never hate. She always said, "Feel sorry for the people who are prejudiced and who practice discrimination because they are weaker. Pray for them that God will help them learn to accept people regardless of their skin color, nationality or race. Someday they will let the Lord touch their hearts. When they do, they will love all people."

My mother's parents

My mother and I developed a very loving relationship. My father and I were close, but it was Mother and I who stayed up late at night reading the Bible and talking about a variety of subjects. That special time became ours. We listened to the radio and when a news program came on the air, we discussed it. When we bought the newspaper, she read that paper from front to back.

Her morning still starts with reading the Bible and then the newspaper. Mother remains committed to her faith and interested in the world around her.

One of her proudest moments came when President Lyndon Johnson invited us to the White House in honor of my performance at the Tchaikovsky Competition in Moscow, Russia.

To Mother, a gracious little black lady from a small town in Iowa, the President's invitation marked a high point in her life.

Mother enjoyed the limousine service, but admitted she was a bit nervous about the dinner. Using my childhood name, she said, "Billy, I don't have any business going there. I won't know what silverware to use."

I tried to reassure her. "Be clever and subtle. Don't start to eat until the head person at your table begins. Watch and see which fork or spoon that person uses. Then do the same."

At dinner that evening, Mother handled everything very well. Of course, she ate very little because she didn't like the food–Estes family standards require all food to be very well done. She took little bites of everything just to be polite. She was so proud to be eating at the White House with the President

Although she never had a day of formal training, Mother was born with a beautiful voice—a gift from God.

that she didn't mind going just a little bit hungry. At dinner, Mother sat with Victor Borge and some other people. She told me later that they had been discussing their oil investments at one point in the conversation.

CLASS OF SERVICE

This is a fast message unless its deferred character is indicated by the proper symbol.

WESTERN U

TELEGRAM

The filing time shown in the date line on domestic telegrams is LOCAL TIME at point of origin. Time at

628A CST NOV 9 68 MA029 CTA030
CT WWYP47 WWZ7 WWZ7 GOVT NL PDB WASHINGTON D
SIMON ESTES, DONT DWR
2502 WOODLAND AVE DES MOINES IOWA
THE PRESIDENT AND MRS. JOHNSON HOPE YOU CAN
AN INFORMAL RECEPTION HONORING THE NATIONAL CC
ARTS ON THURSDAY, NOVEMBER 21, 1968 AT SIX O'C
HOUSE. FORMAL INVITATION FOLLOWS. RSVP
THE SOCIAL SECRETARY THE WHITE HOUSE

21 1968.

When Mother commented, "I have oil on my land, too," the conversation stopped and all attention turned toward her. She continued in a serious tone, "My car leaks all the time in the driveway." Her dinnermates found Mother delightful!

Today, one of the great joys in her life remains knowing things are going well for me, my family, and my career. However, she often tells me she wishes I could perform more in America. "I don't understand why they won't let you sing in this country, Billy. I think it's because you have been a man of principle and have spoken out about the discrimination in the classical world. Remember Jesus' trials. Remember you are a little mortal human being. You have to continue to struggle." She still teaches and encourages me.

A phone call to Mother to tell her how much I appreciate her always highlights my birthdays. "I thank God that He let you give birth to me.

I want you to know I love you very much and I thank you for everything you have done for me. Because of you and Daddy, I am what I am today."

"Billy," she says, "the best you can give your children is to make sure they have a great foundation in the Lord. The Lord is Love."

My mother has endured incredibly hard work, great suffering, and heart-breaking loss. She has grieved the deaths of her first daughter who lived only a few days, her adult daughters Patty and Westella, and her husband.

Her advice to those experiencing heartache is, "Just look to the Lord. I couldn't have made it through any of my hard times without Him. The Lord always brings us through."

In my family, we were very poor economically speaking; however, in terms of respect and love for God and other people, we were extremely wealthly.

My mother lives what's important in life: belief in God, good character, honesty, and respect for others.

Patty

Westella

Erdyne

Dwane

Patty

Patty was a very sweet and caring person who loved people. She was probably the brightest and most talented of us children. Her high school yearbook says, "Many fine qualities, but her voice is her finest." Patty should have been the one to attend The Juilliard School, but New York was far away—both in distance and dollars.

In those days, young women chose careers as nurses, teachers, or secretaries, not as opera singers. After graduating from high school in 1949, Patty graduated from nursing school in Des Moines. She then moved to Ottumwa, Iowa, to work in a hospital and attend the Midwest School of Evangelism where she sang in a quartet. Several Southern churches invited this group to perform. Patty loved singing with her talented friends and was excited about traveling with them.

A southern administrator shattered her dreams when he issued this edict: "Don't bring the colored girl with you." His cruelty totally devastated Patty. She couldn't believe Christians turned her away because of her color. She believed that genuine Christians saw no "color" because God didn't. He accepts and loves all people—regardless of their skin.

None of us had any idea that Patty was depressed. Her depression deepened into despair. Her life, so full of promise, ended when she was 25 due to an overdose of sleeping pills.

Westella

Westella enjoyed people and let them know she cared. She was one of my most enthusiastic fans. She had such great faith in God. Whenever something was troubling or painful, I looked to Westella for help and guidance. I would call her and we'd pray together. Her faith was so deep. I always believed she had a direct line to God.

Westella and our cousin Constance Barnes were killed in a car accident while they were driving back to Des Moines following my Centerville benefit concert on May 13, 1994. In his eulogy at their funeral, our brother Dwane stated that, "A deep faith has been in our family for generations. God has called His children home. We know they are with Jesus, and we know we will see them again."

At the end of the Centerville concert, Mother requested that I sing "Precious Lord, Take My Hand." The first person I saw stand for an ovation at the conclusion of that song was Westella. Since that was the last song Westella and Constance heard me sing, it seemed fitting that I sing it at their funeral. The words of Thomas A. Dorsey's song had been prophetic:

> When my way grows drear', Precious Lord, linger near,
> When my life is almost gone,
> Hear my cry, hear my call, hold my hand, lest I fall;
> Take my hand, Precious Lord, lead me home.

Erdyne

My third sister Erdyne was born in l936, two years before her little brother Billy. She, too, attended Centerville schools and graduated in 1956. Erdyne participated in basketball and a variety of track events, as well as chorus and All-State Choir. After high school, she married and raised seven children.

To this day, she claims Mother punished her for things I did. I can't imagine why she says this since I was so innocent.

In 1965, Erdyne's life was changed forever. She shares her story with the hope it will make a difference for others. Due to heavy drinking, Erdyne developed a very serious alcohol-related illness that led her to a ten-day coma from which she wasn't expected to recover. My mother was sitting outside her hospital room, when a minister came by and asked if he could pray over Erdyne. My mother said yes. After a while he came out and said to my mother, "Tomorrow your daughter will be okay." Before the coma, Erdyne believed in God, but when she regained consciousness, she knew He spared her life because He had a purpose for her.

For 20 years, she has worked with high school students dealing with their behavioral problems. She affirms, "All children need to be loved." She tells them there is no future in alcohol, that they should concentrate on their education, feel pride in themselves, and take and enjoy each day as it comes. Erdyne also devotes her time and abilities to her church and to the Simon Estes South African Youth Chorus (in Des Moines, Iowa, for the 1998–99 school year). Erdyne loves to help people, never turns anybody away, and is kind-hearted—just like our mother and father.

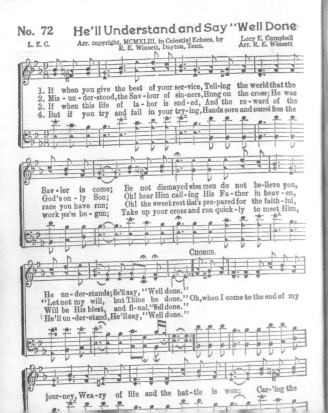

Dwane

Between my junior and senior years in high school, Dwane was born. My father dearly loved this little person and he would be so proud of Dwane today.

Dwane lived in Centerville until I moved him and Mother to Iowa City after Daddy died. We all enjoyed watching Dwane grow up, go to college and start his own family.

Dwane is very musically talented. Mother insists that if he had just kept up with piano lessons, he could be my accompanist.

He works at an area education agency in Iowa, utilizing his computer skills.

Dwane enjoys being a father to Katie, his beautiful daughter, a high school student who is blessed with a fine voice herself. Dwane also is a loving husband to a lady he met in high school. Too shy to ask her out then, he waited 25 years. They were married in July of 1998.

Dwane is very religious and loves the Lord. He praises His name daily.

Simon Lamont Estes

I was born at home on March 2, 1938, with Dr. Charles Brummitt present for the delivery. He and my father grew up together in the same small Missouri town. My mother explained that to save their figures, the white women hired black women to nurse their babies, and that my grandmother had been little Charlie Brummitt's wet nurse.

He moved to Centerville after medical school and became our family doctor. The cycle of survival had come full circle; now we were as dependent on Dr. Brummitt to maintain our health as he had been on my grandmother to sustain him.

My father wanted to name me William or Billy, but my mother preferred "Simon" as a tribute to my father. After much discussion, Mother had her way and I was christened Simon Lamont Estes. However, I was nicknamed Billy to avoid the confusion of having two Simons.

Erdyne and "the scrawny little boy" look for the photographer's birdie.

"Billy" remained my name until third grade when I wanted the more grown-up name of Simon. While classmates accepted my new name, most of my family still call me "Billy."

I spent the first three years of my life at 910 East Jackson. That little house, scarcely big enough for a couple, became home to a family of six. The rooms were quite small, the largest measuring 8' by 12'. We had a living room, a bedroom for my parents, a kitchen, and an all-purpose room used for eating and playing. My sisters slept in the all-purpose room and I slept in the living room. A potbelly stove produced heat for one room with only a teasing of heat for the rest of the house. My three sisters claimed most of the space in that house because I was a scrawny little boy who didn't take up much room—I reminded them of that fact whenever possible.

We were very active children who filled that house with laughter and joy. When I was about three, a photographer came to our home and fascinated me as he set up his camera. When he pulled a black cloth over his head, I couldn't understand why he was hiding. I wasn't sure what this picture-taking business was all about.

When the man told me to "look at the birdie," I was really perplexed. I looked all around the room, but I couldn't see any bird—in a cage or anywhere else. The photographer repeated that phrase three or four times. I did my best to find the bird, and then I became frustrated.

Even as a three-year-old, my logical mind told me there was no bird in the room. To this day, when I know the facts, I become frustrated if others use illogical tactics with me.

That little house on Jackson Street still stands today, and I hope the families who lived there since were as happy and blessed as we were.

When I was four years old, we moved to a larger house on 21st Street. Many whites refused to sell property to blacks in those days, but we bought this house from a white farmer. He knew my father was an honorable man and appreciated

For Erdyne, Westella, and me, our second home on 21st Street seemed like a palace, especially after our father lovingly remodeled it.

the difficulties my father faced in trying to find a bigger house for his family. They worked out a price of about $1200.

I've been told by my mother that when the farmer's son discovered his father had sold the place to colored people, he was furious, thinking white people would have paid twice as much. His father took the position that Simon Estes was a decent man with a fine family; he had given his word to him and he would be the buyer.

We were one of the few black families in Centerville for whom it was financially possible to own a home. My father must have had great faith in his ability to provide for us, because $1200 was a huge debt to incur in those days.

Our new house seemed like a palace because it had six rooms. Over the years, my father remodeled the entire house. The downstairs boasted a kitchen, living room, dining room, and a bedroom for my parents. My three sisters shared the two upstairs bedrooms; I slept downstairs in the dining room.

Mother kept the inside spotless, which was not easy. During the hot dusty summers, open windows provided the only air conditioning.

Dust rolled in from the street and, to make matters worse, the well went dry. In these dry spells, any movement from the street sent clouds of dust creeping under the windowsills and doors, coating everything. Our only relief came when the city oiled the street and thunderstorms calmed the dust.

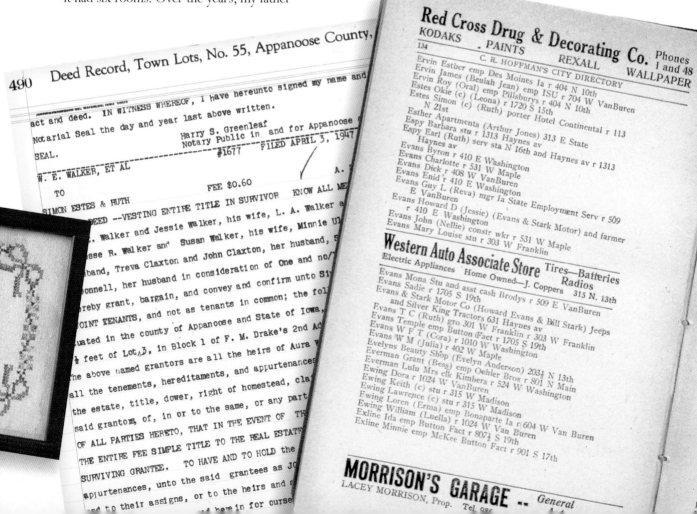

My Own Family

My three beautiful daughters are the most important people in my life—I am really blessed to be the father of Jennifer Barbara, Lynne Ashley, and Tiffany Joy. They participate in a wealth of activities—Jennifer plays the flute while Lynne and Tiffany take harp lessons. They all three ski and play tennis. Jennifer ice-skates with a precision team and is also active in scouting. All of these activities keep my children healthy and enthusiastic about life.

When I am traveling, I call my daughters every day. All three are very close to each other, which pleases me. I have taught them to be kind, caring and compassionate. I believe that the family unit is the strongest support we have in our daily lives. We pray at mealtimes and before they go to bed at night. I tell them, as my mother told me, that God is the One source of love and strength that will never disappoint them. I hope He will always be a part of their lives.

My family has undergone a very sad change during the last years because my wife and I are no longer married. In that I do not advocate divorce, I was willing to continue the marriage for the sake of our children and to maintain the family unit. My wife insisted on the divorce, and I reluctantly agreed.

Before we married, she agreed religion would be an important part of our marriage, but she gradually moved away from that commitment. This, and other unresolved problems, resulted in the deterioration of our relationship. Our differences on an increasing number of levels were disappointing. She did not want me to "interfere" with her way of bringing up the children. Again, I deferred to her wishes but will always regret that Jennifer, Lynne, and Tiffany's education has not been a shared experience and responsibility since what I have always wanted my daughters to know is the importance of spirituality, values, principles, morality, and honesty. However, my former wife is the lady I chose to marry and we have together three lovely daughters. I especially want Jennifer, Lynne, and Tiffany to know that their mother will always have a special place in my heart. When communication breaks down and the emotional and spiritual bonds are broken, the relationship tragically comes to an end. Although my wife and I are no longer married, the welfare of our daughters is the primary focus in my life.

My children are more important to me than any career or social life. My first choice is to be at home with my three daughters.

My daughters, Jennifer the oldest, Lynne, and Tiffany, the youngest

Growing Up in Iowa

During my world travels, people often ask, "Where are you from?"

When I tell them Iowa, the usual reaction is "Where's that?" or they confuse it with Ohio.

Next they ask me, "How did you get to be a world-class opera singer?" That takes a little longer to answer because I have often asked myself that question and, even after 35 years of professional singing, I don't have all the answers.

However, I believe that it comes down to three factors. First is the gift. I inherited a musical gift from my mother, but the true giver of the gift is the Lord Himself. It is my responsibility to develop that gift.

Second, regardless of how talented we might be, we need both divine help and help from our fellow human beings. I have been blessed by many wonderful people who have befriended, encouraged, and supported me.

Third, we are to love one another and live in peace. This has been a challenge for me to practice because of the prejudice I have experienced due to the color of my skin.

A mix of people and experiences has molded and refined my values and beliefs. They shaped my mission to share my abilities and my accomplishments, and to make a difference for others.

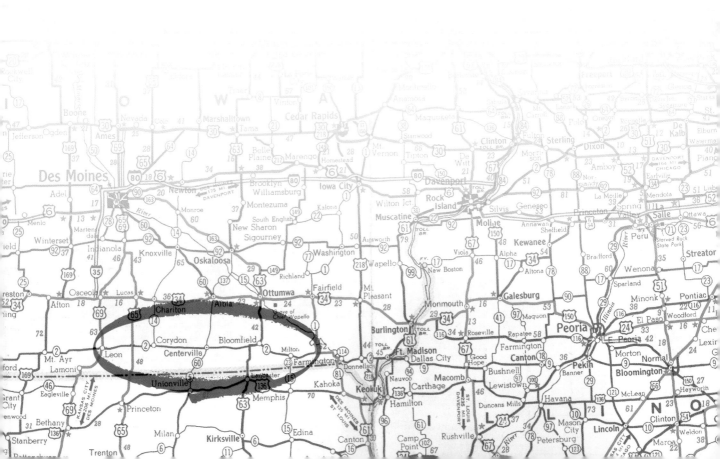

Neighbors. In Centerville, we had some wonderful neighbors like Blanche Connor who didn't have a prejudiced bone in her body. She treated us all so kindly, especially when our well ran dry during hot spells. Knowing how hard it was to be without water in the summer, Blanche let us carry water from her well to our house. That way my mother could do the laundry or the dishes or we could take Saturday night baths.

In contrast, one of our neighbors was not so kind. He was a terrible racist who always referred to us as "the coloreds" or "little black niggers." He swore and shook his fist at my sisters and me (Dwane had not been born yet) if we bothered him. He poisoned our dog after it wandered into his yard. Legally he had a case, but he could have solved the problem in other ways. Our dog was only a mutt, but we loved him and cried for days over his death. Our neighbor had no sympathy for us. He didn't even consider us to be human beings, but "little black niggers" who had no feelings.

Prejudice didn't keep his wife from taking advantage of us whenever possible. One branch of our cherry tree draped over the fence between his property and ours. After his wife helped herself to the cherries on their side, she reached over and filled her pail with those on our side. Mother could see her early in the morning picking cherries as she sang "Can you bake a cherry pie?" Years later when that woman faded into sickness and old age, guess who helped her? My mother, of course, who was certain of how God wanted her to treat others, regardless of their attitudes toward us. Mother practices what she preaches.

The Garden. During my childhood, most people cultivated their World War II victory gardens as a patriotic duty; we had ours as a means of survival.

We worked hard in that garden and it gave us food we couldn't afford to buy, like fresh corn, lettuce, green beans, and potatoes. We had cherry and apple trees, gooseberry and raspberry bushes, and grape vines. We also raised chickens for eggs and meat. Mother canned some of the fruits and vegetables and stored the rest in our underground cellar.

The grocery store. At times, we needed to buy staples from the grocery store. Mr. Shallcross ran the little store on the corner of 18th and Maple, just a few blocks from our house. When times were hard for my parents, he let them open a charge account to buy the bread, milk, and flour our family needed. He trusted my father to repay him when he could. Mr. Shallcross extended this courtesy to other black families, too.

Mr. Shallcross was always so kind to us children. Some of the kids stole candy from him, but I never did; I couldn't do that to such a good person.

Sometimes Mr. Shallcross would let me charge a penny or two of candy, which was like having Santa in the neighborhood grocery all year long.

Once, I overheard one of the store clerks objecting to Mr. Shallcross extending credit to black families. In his clipped British accent, Mr. Shallcross told the clerk that blacks are human beings and should be treated as such.

I will never forget that conversation or his kindness to our family.

Simple living. Taking a bath on Saturday night involved a great deal of work. No wonder it happened only once a week! We pumped water from the well, heated it on the stove, and poured it into the galvanized washtub on the kitchen floor. The whole process took most of Saturday evening.

Washing clothes was even more time-consuming. Since we didn't own an electric washing machine until I was in high school, my mother used a process similar to the baths to wash our clothes. She hauled water from the well, heated it on the stove, and poured the water into the washtub. She then used a scrub board to get the dirt out of the clothes.

Because we didn't have a dryer, she hung the clothes on a line outdoors. In the winter, those clothes came off the line frozen stiff as boards and still damp.

During Iowa's hot summers, we worried about keeping our food cool. We relied on our ice box, precursor to the refrigerator. A big hunk of ice inside the ice box kept everything from spoiling. As the ice melted, we needed to replace it quite often. That was the ice man's job. In his horse-drawn wagon, he made the rounds of the neighborhoods several times a week.

Each family placed a color-coded card in the window so the delivery man knew what size ice block to deliver. Each side of the square card had a different color: red for 25 pounds, white for 50, blue for 75, and black for 100 pounds. We displayed the side with the amount we wanted at the top so the ice man could read our request from the street. I doubt we could afford 100 pounds, but the golden opportunity to be like the rich people was always there on one side of the card.

What a treat it was in the summer when the ice man came down our street! He gave us little chips of broken ice and we sucked on them until they were gone—just like candy. In the hot humid summers, those ice chips were almost as much of a treat as ice cream.

The Black Lizard. No one in my group of friends had a car as old as my father's. I called it the Black Lizard in hopes it would live up to the quickness of its namesake. The Black Lizard was a different sort of car. Slow to start, once it got past 50, it never stopped accelerating!

Character building. Like most children, my sisters, brother, and I were not perfect as we grew up. Sometimes we needed to be disciplined. Neither of my parents believed in punishment for punishment's sake, and never resorted to spanking without a good reason.

The New Air-Conditioned Refrigerator

25

Display with Amount Wanted on Top

PURE ICE COMPANY
PHONE 169

It is our desire at all times to render the kind of service you are entitled to. Therefore we request that you notify us of any inattention or unbecoming conduct on the part of our employees.

Please Read Message on Back of This Card

50

75

Permanent Drains—No Drip Pans to Em

My father spanked me only once after I lied to him. My cousin Kenneth and I were playing "African warrior" with the other neighborhood kids. We had fashioned spears from sticks and were throwing them at one another. I hurled my stick a little harder than I intended, and it hit Kenneth in the eye. He screamed at the top of his lungs.

Kenneth's parents were visiting with my parents in the house. When they heard Kenneth crying, they all streamed out of the house shouting, "What happened?"

I quickly volunteered, "Kenneth fell and the stick went into his eye."

Kenneth was in too much pain at the time to refute my statement. My father calmly scooped Kenneth into his arms, gently put him in the car with my uncle and quickly drove to the doctor's office.

I was a nervous wreck the whole time they were gone. I was worried about Kenneth and terrified that I had blinded him, but I was also hoping that he would not tell our fathers the true story. Unfortunately for me, when he calmed down, he reported the facts.

When my father came home, he very calmly said, "Son, come here." I knew my number was up, and slowly walked to him.

"I'm gonna spank you, not because you hit Kenneth in the eye with a stick, because that was an accident," he said in measured tones. "I'm gonna spank you because you lied to me, and when I finish, you will never lie to me again." He was right.

My mother was more generous with her discipline, but she wasn't as strong as my

I called my father's car the black Lizard in hopes it would live up to the quickness of its namesake.

father. Her spankings didn't last very long either, because when I called on the Lord to forgive this woman who was spanking her innocent lamb, I made her laugh and the punishment ended.

The foundation. Whenever we children came home from school, my mother was always there to greet us. She prepared all of our meals, provided us with a hug when needed and with guidance. Any free time my father had, he spent with us.

Television sets became household items when I was in junior high school, but a set was beyond our budget. The radio was our source of entertainment, and we also spent time with each other—talking, playing, singing and praying.

Centerville. Centerville, the county seat of Appanoose County, Iowa, was named after an early citizen whose name was actually spelled *Senter*. Its unique and majestic county courthouse was built before the turn of the century. The courthouse square sits in the center of

town, surrounded by a large lawn. In 1940, Centerville's official population was 8,413.

When I was a boy, our main family entertainment was driving "uptown" to the southeast corner of the square on Saturday evening. This unusual reference is legendary in Centerville, because no matter what direction anyone lived from the square, it was always "uptown." Certain sides of the square were more prestigious than others; we chose the south side. If we were lucky, we got a parking spot right in front of Elgin's Clothing Store where we watched the people go by as they shopped and visited. Stores stayed open until 9:00 PM on Saturdays, the day the farmers came to town. It was a wonderful way to feel part of the town and its social scene.

Friends. As a young boy, I had such happy times playing with friends who were a mixture of white and black. Color didn't matter to us. Our yards were deep jungles teeming with tigers and other wild animals. Fields were immense, as big as continents. The hill going up to the

Waggoner house from the cemetery was like a mountain and their house was a castle. The first time I returned to Centerville as an adult, I thought I was in the wrong town! That hill, the immense fields, and the house had shrunk drastically. My imagination was the only thing that had been gigantic.

My friends included Jon Hicks ("Hicksey"), Ron James, Darryl Coatney, Floyd Brooks (whom I called "Flu Flu Fleet, the Sheik of Araby"), Jimmy Downing, Joe Barnes, and my cousin Johnny Edward Powell. Jon Hicks, the best talker of the group, once convinced Ron and me that we needed to fight. We had no idea why, but we were "duking" it out when Ron caught me with a right to the jaw and knocked me out for a few seconds. I hit the ground, my head cleared, I jumped up, and came face to face with Jack Edling. Our coach had been watching.

"That's enough, you boys," he ordered. "Shake hands and go on home."

Ron and I shook hands and walked toward home as if nothing had happened. Suddenly, Ron asked, "Why were we fighting?"

I couldn't remember. The incident helped me realize the importance of thinking for myself, sometimes taking what people say with a grain of salt, and living in peace with others.

Floyd Brooks and I rode bikes together as often as we could. I saved for my bike by working as a substitute paper carrier and doing other odd jobs, and I was very proud of it. One summer day, Flu Flu suggested we ride our bikes down Maple Street, just a block away. We had sailed down Maple and turned onto an uphill dirt trail when a large tree jumped directly into my path. I tried to ride my bike up its trunk, but within seconds, I found myself in a heap on the ground. Alarmed, Flu Flu stood over me shouting, "Simon, your bicycle is a mess!"

"Forget about the bike," I gasped, "what about me?" I had cracked my head on the tree and had the wind knocked out of me.

"Simon, look at your bicycle!" I looked and

I spent many happy childhood days playing with my older cousin, Johnny Powell.

wished I hadn't. If that bike had been a horse, we would have shot it. My prized possession was a mangled mess; it was totaled. My sorrow ricocheted between my loss and my aching body.

Flu Flu and I often played in the Oakland Cemetery just two blocks from home. One day when we were about ten years old, we had played among the tombstones until it started to get dark. This was one place we didn't want to be when the sun went down. Just as we crossed a little creek, Flu Flu shouted, "A snake!"

The panic in his voice told me it must be 16 feet long and dine exclusively on small boys. We ran for our lives! As we crossed that stream, one of my shoes stuck in the muck. I knew the snake had my shoe. Well, it was all his! As we raced home, my common sense returned. I knew I should go back and get that shoe, but the thought of the snake with my shoe in its mouth terrified me and kept me going toward home.

My parents noticed I was missing a shoe the minute I walked in the house. They were very upset; that was my only pair of shoes and the next day was Sunday. No way would my parents allow me to attend church barefoot. My dear patient father took me by the hand and led me back to the snake-infested cemetery where we found the shoe, still stuck in the goo where I lost it. At home, Daddy washed the shoe, put it in the oven to dry, and later rubbed it with Vaseline® to soften the leather. It looked fine and I wore it to church with no problem. As an adult, I realize how dismayed my father must have been when I appeared in the living room minus that shoe. He certainly couldn't afford another pair of shoes, but he was calm, patient, and loving throughout the entire episode.

More character building. On a lazy summer day, a friend and I walked "uptown" to Allen's news shop to look over the latest comics. As usual, I didn't have any money but he had a dime or two. The Allens always allowed us to look over the latest comics, knowing that most often we couldn't afford to buy even one.

As I looked through a comic book, out of the corner of my eye, I saw my friend roll two comics together to look like one. He sauntered

to the counter, paid for one, and left the store. I followed him.

Outside, I grabbed his arm. "You took two comics!"

"No, I didn't," he said nonchalantly. "I only took one. I bought the other one." He explained how this ruse worked and how he always got two comics for the price of one.

His matter-of-fact explanation made the two-for-one deal sound good. I couldn't wait to try my hand at this new way of shopping. I knew it wasn't right, but the thought of two comics for the price of one was too great a temptation and I had a dime that begged to be spent.

I walked to Allen's as soon as it opened. After looking at the selection, I proceeded to roll two comics into one à la my friend, pay for the one, and leave the store. The minute I walked out the door, my conscience began to bother me. I had been taught that a good Christian boy did not steal, especially a good Christian Estes boy. My conscience bothered me all day, pushing me to do the right thing.

I had trouble sleeping that night. How was I going to atone for my crime? I couldn't tell Mr. Allen that I had stolen from him. He might not let me in the store again. Worse, he might tell my parents and I knew what they thought of stealing. I could be in big trouble. After agonizing over my problem for hours, I came up with a solution. I would tell Mr. Allen I had bought a comic thinking it was a ten-cent variety only to discover when I reached home that it was a 25-cent comic. Then I'd pay him the difference.

After a very long night, I walked to Allen's and gave Mr. Allen my fifteen cents along with my explanation and apologies. I now had an empty pocket and a clear conscience.

Twenty-five cents was a large amount of money to me. In all, I had given him the 20 cents I owed him for the two comics and a nickel to absolve my sin. I vowed never to steal again.

One day when I had the extraordinary amount of five cents, I went with my cousin Johnny Powell to buy an ice cream cone at Dawkins Cafe. We paid for our cones and sat down at the counter stools to enjoy them.

Wiping his hands on a towel, the owner asked, "Did you boys want something else?"

"No thank you," we said.

"You don't want anything else?"

Lick, lick, smack, lick. "No."

"Why are you sitting here?"

We were just seven or eight years old and had no idea we were sitting in a whites-only cafe.

"Do you want some ice cream to take home?"

"No." We continued eating our cones.

With an edge in his voice he said, "Then you'll have to leave. You can't stay in here."

I looked around the small cafe and noticed other people sitting and eating. I didn't understand. "Those people are eating in here. You aren't asking them to leave."

"Colored people can't eat in here," he said, emphasizing each word. "Get out right now."

"But my Uncle Oakey cleans this place," I informed him. I thought my uncle had a very important job and this man should be impressed. He wasn't. In a gruff voice, he told us that my uncle didn't count and he would fire him if we said anything about being told to leave. Terrified, we ran out of the restaurant.

I'd always thought my family couldn't eat a full meal at Dawkins or any other cafe in town because we were too poor and only rich people ate out. That we were "coloreds" and therefore not allowed in any cafe was a new concept to Johnny and me.

As my horizons broadened, I learned I couldn't swim in the afternoons at the pool. I couldn't play golf at the country club, and when I did, I was asked to leave. I later found out my father could only stand in the doorway to a drug store when he was asked to run errands for hotel patrons. That was life as "colored" in many towns.

Grade school days—when my classmates and I became aware of our color differences

Early in grade school, two of my white class-mates had a conversation that has stayed with me to this day. One girl asked another, "Do you like Simon because he is colored or does that even matter?"

Without hesitation, the second answered, "I like him no matter what color he is."

"I feel the same way," the first girl replied.

Although that exchange couldn't have lasted more than a few seconds, I realized they were aware of my color; it made me more aware of the differences between my white classmates and me.

Racial issues often registered with me, but I didn't understand them because I was so young. One day, I came home from school and asked my parents, "What's a black nigger? Why do they

call me a 'dirty black nigger'?" I was confused.

Although it was painful to hear the names I was called, my parents explained without anger that "nigger" is a bad word some people use to describe us. "Billy, don't worry. Just love those people who call you names and pray for them."

When you are seven or eight years old, that is very hard to do. However, I have tried to live by my parents' wisdom and example.

Elementary school. When I was in grade school, I was the scrawniest little boy in town. My cousin Marion Estes Waller described me as a "coat hanger with teeth." Every time we had high winds, my mother worried that I would blow away. She gave my sisters strict orders to walk me home on extremely windy days.

During one fierce wind storm, my sisters

arrived home from school without me. Alarmed, Mother asked why they hadn't brought me home. They had no answers nor were they particularly concerned. (I would bet there were times when they hoped their pesky little brother *would* blow away.)

Worried, Mother went in search of her little matchstick child. She found me with my arms wrapped around a light pole, pinned to it by the wind. I was afraid I would be there all night in the cold and dark clinging to that pole. I was so happy to see her. She put me under her coat so I was out of the wind and, clutching me tightly, she took me home.

When I was in second grade, the teacher called my mother to school for a conference about her little Billy and his behavior. I was a typical mischievous, energetic seven-year-old. According to the teacher, I made the kids laugh with my antics, making it hard for them to concentrate, and making the teacher's job difficult.

At home, Mother demanded an explanation. "I do it to make the other children happy," I explained in all honesty and sincerity. "I don't do it for myself. I do it for them." That was the truth. I remember telling jokes and acting silly because I wanted them to be happy. When they felt good, I felt good. My mother wasn't pleased with my charitable acts and told me I would behave in class and make the teacher happy, not the kids.

One of the most coveted jobs for a sixth-grader was that of a safety patrol crossing guard

As a typical energetic seven-year-old, I liked to make the kids laugh.

who helped the other children cross the street safely on their way to and from school. They wore white straps across their chests so motorists could tell the difference between the students and the patrol. Patrol members stopped cars and trucks by raising their hands—what fun, what responsibility!

When teachers asked for volunteers, all of us raised our hands high. To my recollection, no one of my color received the honor of being on the school safety patrol. In those days, many white people believed that black people could not accept responsibility. If the opportunity was never offered to us, how could we learn? How could we demonstrate our sense of responsibility? None of us were "teacher's pets" who were chosen to hand out papers, erase

blackboards, run errands, or serve on the safety patrol. To have been chosen for anything would have made us feel special.

Like every other boy in my sixth grade class, I had a crush on the beautiful Miss Curl. I thought she was Miss America. She was gorgeous and she was so nice. It was hard to concentrate when she was reading or talking to the class because her beauty mesmerized me. I was always on my best behavior in Miss Curl's class. That was one grade I would have been willing to repeat.

All of us were afraid of THE PRINCIPAL. I remember quite well the first time I was called to her office. The exact infraction I've forgotten, but I am certain it must have been serious to warrant a summons by THE PRINCIPAL. The walk down the hall to her office was endless— like those in your dreams where you walk and walk because your goal keeps rolling away from you. With each trembling step, I recalled stories told by friends who survived their visit to THE PRINCIPAL'S OFFICE.

Cautiously, I opened her door and stepped into her presence. She stood at least 17 feet tall and the desk she sat behind was the size of a battleship. After she reviewed my "crime," I recall her saying, "If you are ever sent to this office again, I will put you in the vault where there is very little air and you could suffocate."

That comment is seared into my memory. What an awful thing to tell a child! She frightened me so badly that I vowed to avoid doing anything that would land me back in her office.

Unfortunately, I did return, but my trips back were rare.

That principal handled a problem with my sister Erdyne in a very unorthodox manner. Erdyne had been accused of some wrongdoing and, as punishment, the principal made two other girls come into her office and hit Erdyne with their fists. Those girls did what they were told not because they had any hard feelings against Erdyne, but because they were too terrified to defy the principal.

My parents were furious when Erdyne told them what happened. They went to school to discuss that method of discipline. Although it was not used on my sister again, the principal did not apologize to my parents.

High School. When we were in high school, my friends and I enjoyed going to the Majestic Theater. Because of the unwritten segregation laws of that time, my white friends sat downstairs close to the screen while the "coloreds" had to sit upstairs by the smelly men's restroom.

When I was a high school senior, the most powerful men in the world were Truman, Eisenhower, Churchill, Stalin, and Loren Karth, our head custodian.

Our area was nicknamed "the crow's nest" because of our skin color.

One Sunday night in 1956 when I was a high school senior, my friends decided this was the time to integrate the movie theater. As I started for the balcony, one of the group said, "Why are you going usptairs, Si?"

"To find a place to sit."

"Not tonight. You're going to sit downstairs with us."

"No way, guys." I protested. "Are you nuts? Coloreds have to sit upstairs. We'll be kicked out for sure." I was not brave enough to disobey an unwritten rule of society, and I didn't want to tangle with the manager.

My friends insisted I was going to sit downstairs with them no matter what.

Reluctantly, I followed them into the forbidden region of the main floor. Halfway down the aisle, the manager appeared behind us. "Where do you think you're going?" he asked, looking right at me.

"We're going to see the show," said one of my friends as if nothing was wrong.

The manager shook his head. "He's going back upstairs. Coloreds don't sit downstairs with the whites." Turning to face me he said, "Now you get upstairs."

I turned to go, but my friends stood their ground. "No, he's not. He's staying right here. If he doesn't, we're going to tell our dads." This was a powerful threat because most of their fathers were businessmen and the theaters relied heavily on their advertising.

One of the guys nudged me and, despite being scared to death, I stayed with the group and we all sat down.

After a few minutes, the impact of the situation hit me. I was sitting downstairs like white folks. My mind jumped with excitement. "You can't smell the toilets! Look at that screen! You're right here with the action!" I couldn't wait to tell other "coloreds" what life was like on the ground floor of the Majestic and that they, too, could sit there. What my friends did for me was very courageous because, in those days, adults and rules of society were seldom challenged by the younger generation.

Throughout my school years, I was always frightened when we got our report cards every six weeks. I knew I would be in trouble if I got a "C." My mother wanted me to earn only "A" and "B" marks because my parents knew the value of an education. They taught us to be responsible and work hard in school.

When I was in high school, the most powerful men in the world were Harry Truman, Dwight Eisenhower, Winston Churchill, Joseph Stalin, and Loren Karth, our head custodian. The gym floor was his pride and joy. At the end of any event, he roped off the floor and stood guard. No one dared put a toe on Loren's floor.

During junior college, 1956–1957, I worked for Loren. Work I did, but I also learned many important lessons from him, one of the most important being that when you did a job, you did it right the first time and you did it well.

Loren also hired my friend Jim Galloway. One of us thought it would be a good idea to bring a radio and listen to music while we worked.

It wasn't long before Loren heard our music and confiscated the radio, saying, "You can't work and listen to the radio at the same time."

When we did have our radio, I tried to teach Jim how to talk "jive," so we would be washing and mopping, dancing and jiving. Picture two skinny 18-year-olds bopping around while they mopped the floor! We were cool, man, but Loren thought we were too happy-go-lucky. He would point to me and say, "Estes, you'll never amount to a hill of beans."

However, Loren did trust me enough to give me a key to the inside doors of the school building. If he worked on Saturday morning, he would be away until Monday morning, providing what several of us considered a great opportunity to hone our basketball skills. Since my key opened the inside but not the outside doors, I propped open a window in the locker room on Saturday morning so we could get in later. Once we made it inside the school, my key opened the gym. We had some great games on Saturday afternoons before we were caught.

Loren knew immediately who let everyone in. "Simon, you're fired. You are no longer working here," he announced.

I needed that job. I felt sick. In desperation, I went to E. W. Fannon, the Superintendent of Schools, to plead my case. "You know I lost my job. I let the other guys into the gym. We were just playing basketball. We didn't hurt a thing."

E.W. didn't say a word. He just looked at me. I continued to babble, "Isn't it better that we were in there than on the streets?"

In his incredibly deep voice that seemed to rumble up from his toes, he said, "I'll have a talk with Loren." I got my job back and I never crossed Loren again.

Mr. Fannon usually scared most students and teachers. After all, he was the Superintendent, a man of power and importance. However, he always had time to talk, not *to* me, but *with* me. And it wasn't just during my years in high school. Several times when I returned home from college, I visited E.W. He always encouraged me to continue my education and make something of myself. It was quite a morale booster and an honor to know the Superintendent of Schools believed in me.

During my high school years, I tried several sports including basketball, football, and track. I was too small for football, but that didn't stop me. I was fairly short in high school, but I still managed to play a good game of basketball. Track was my favorite. With my long legs, the high jump was my specialty.

Coach Bill Jerome, a hometown boy who returned after college to teach and coach in the high school, was an excellent role model. Truly "color blind," he looked at the whole person and treated all his students fairly. He helped me learn to give 110 percent, especially on defense because that's where games are won. I also learned that sometimes 110 percent is not enough.

Coach Jerome also taught me the value of anticipation—not only in basketball or football, but in all aspects of life. He wanted us to be alert to potential pitfalls and problems that might arise in any situation. "Estes—anticipate!" I still rely on his lessons.

I received a fine education in the Centerville schools. Beyond the incidents of discrimination, I deeply respected the teachers who treated students fairly and with equal concern and regard. I appreciate the opportunities these people and the school system offered, and the positive ways they influenced my life.

Earning Money. When I was growing up, every penny counted. My father and I found endless and various ways to make money. We collected rags and pieces of metal in gunny sacks and sold them to a local businessman.

When needed at the Continental Hotel, I helped my father carry salesmen's bags to their rooms. People usually tipped us a dime. As soon as we made enough money, we quickly

E. W. Fannon, Superintendent of Schools, always had time to talk with me.

basketball days: "Estes—anticipate!"

called my mother. Then she bought food so we had enough to eat that evening.

My father and I also cleaned the Majestic movie theater together, picking up trash and mopping the floors. Sometimes, I was lucky enough to find a dropped nickel or penny on the main floor.

My first paying job was as a substitute carrier for the hometown paper. Because I was "colored," I couldn't have my own route, so I worked for a friend who was a regular carrier.

I carried the papers each day after school for the grand sum of 50 cents a week. I gave a dime to each of my sisters (Dwane hadn't been born yet) and kept 20 cents for myself.

That newspaper route helped me develop social skills, money skills, responsibility, and physical fitness—all in all, a wonderful experience.

Soon after that, *The Des Moines Register and Tribune* gave me my own paper route. We all enjoyed the benefit of a free subscription to the paper, especially Mother.

When I was 12, I switched from the media to aesthetics. I shined shoes and mopped floors at Sconzo's Barber Shop. When I finished, those shoes and floors were a work of art!

Frank Sconzo owned this shop and employed his brother Joe, whose great sense of humor kept me laughing all day—quite a feat because I worked long days from 8:00 AM until 9:30 PM. On many Saturdays, I took only fifteen-minute lunch and supper breaks, then hurried back to work. All afternoon, I shined endless pairs of shoes. When the shop closed at 9:00 PM, I mopped the floors so everything was ready for Monday morning.

Most of Sconzo's customers were regulars and I knew them all. One of my favorites was Mr. Gavronsky—a generous man, a great tipper, and the epitome of good manners. He always treated me with respect and was so pleasant to me.

Not all my customers were as congenial. One afternoon as a man sat down for his shoeshine, he said, "Hey boy, I want you to shine my shoes and when you do, make that rag pop to the rhythm of the music." As a radio played on the back counter, my mind was only half on the music, but his comment struck a discordant note and captured my attention.

Appalled, I didn't say a word. I had started working on his shoes as soon as he sat down, but I stopped. I turned to the man sitting next to him and began working on the customer's shoes.

"Hey, boy, you haven't finished with my shoes yet," the first man complained.

"I'm not going to finish your shoes," I replied. "I'm not a clown. I am here to work, not to entertain you or anybody else."

His face reddened with anger. "You get that soap off my shoes, boy!"

"Not until you apologize."

"Listen, boy, I won't apologize to you. Now get that soap off my shoes right now!" As I continued to clean and polish the other man's shoes, the first man complained angrily to Mr. Sconzo. "Frank, this boy won't take the saddle soap off my shoes and they're all wet."

Mr. Sconzo put down his scissors and comb. Wiping his hands, he came around the chair and asked, "What's the problem, Simon? What's wrong with you?"

Remaining calm, I answered, "This man insulted me. He wants me to pop my rag to the rhythm of the music and entertain him like a clown."

Frank frowned. The situation put him in an awkward position. He could understand why I'd stopped shining the man's shoes, but he hated to have a customer upset. "Oh, come on, Simon," he said, trying to smooth things over. "Clean his shoes and get on with your work."

"Not until he apologizes." I was adamant.

Raising his voice a little, Frank said, "Wipe off those shoes, Simon."

I refused. "No. I will not. If he apologizes, I will gladly finish his shoes, but until then, I won't."

After several uncomfortable minutes, the man cleared his throat and, in a low, quiet voice, mumbled an apology.

I think he realized I was not backing down and he would sit there with wet shoes until he did.

Even though I worked in the barbershop, I couldn't get my hair cut there. No shop allowed "coloreds" to have their hair cut on the premises, because most white customers didn't want a hair cut with the same scissors and comb used on a colored man's hair. Usually my father or my Uncle Johnny Powell cut my hair at someone's house. Since I was working for Frank, I asked him if he would do me a favor and cut my hair. He agreed to cut it for me after work when the shop closed.

"Simon," he said, "you must never let anybody know that I cut your hair because I could lose business if anyone found out."

He stepped to the front of the shop, pulled the blinds down, and pushed them in around the window. He then tried the lock on the door to make sure it was secure. When he was certain no one could see in through cracks in the blinds or walk in the door, he cut my hair. His heart was in the right place.

I was lucky to have that job at Sconzo's. The money was good, but I would have liked to work in a place like the Owl Drug Store or Elgin's Clothing Store. I used to dream about working in one of those stores where I could wear my good clothes and meet all kinds of people. Instead I polished shoes with my hands and a rag soaked in shoe polish. When I left work, I smelled like shoe polish and my hands were stained an even darker color.

One summer during high school, I had a job at the Iowa Southern Utilities Company as a substitute for the regular night watchman who was on vacation. I made the rounds with my set of keys, punching the time clock to record my trips around the building. I also had a few janitorial duties. In my mind, I was important—I was like a policeman protecting the Iowa Southern Utilities Company.

That job meant so much to me. All that responsibility made me proud and happy, and my parents were in seventh heaven to think that their son had such an important job. This company trusted me, a black person, with this prestigious job. To scrub those floors and empty the wastebaskets and ashtrays at Iowa Southern was a big deal in my mind.

While discrimination is nation-wide and not unique to Centerville, it exists and these experiences are part of who I am. Far more abundant are the positive school and community people and experiences that helped shape my values, morals, and character. Centerville holds a very special, very warm place in my heart.

I will always remember and be grateful to those who helped, encouraged, and believed in the "matchstick boy."

A restored section of the hotel barbershop where I once shined shoes

015107

Continental Hotel
CENTERVILLE, IOWA

015107

NENTAL HOTEL, CENTERVILLE, IOWA.

*Items from the Continental Hotel
where both my father and I worked*

Singing in Centerville

Beginning in Centerville, expanding to Iowa City, then on to Berlin and the world, key people and experiences helped me develop my gift.

Church. I don't remember a point at which I "became" interested in music because music was always a part of my life. My family's proudest possession was a battered old upright piano that Mother or Patty played. We'd all gather around the piano and sing hymns, harmonizing as best we could and entertaining ourselves for hours. Maintenance was never a problem because if a key went out of tune or something broke off, we just ignored it.

Our church gave us the first opportunity to sing outside our home. When I was seven or eight, I began to sing solos at the church. Sometimes our family piled into the car and drove to other nearby churches to sing. The joy of traveling and singing together was a wonderful experience.

Grade School. In elementary school, I took violin lessons from patient Mr. Minckler. Although he must have known from the start that I had little interest in the violin, he always treated me kindly. I'm certain he hoped I would break a finger or two playing ball and not return, but he never discouraged me.

I also took piano lessons for several months until marble season arrived and my mother realized I was not practicing.

the church where I first sang solos

"Billy," she said, "we're not paying the 25 cents a week for piano lessons if you're not going to practice. Either practice or play marbles."

Predictably, I opted for the marbles. Today, I regret that decision because I can play only a few chords on the piano.

I sang a few solos in elementary school and made straight A's in music class. Miss Clark, our music teacher, always made us sing scales before we opened that green music book and sang the fun songs. It was easy for me to carry a tune, and I always felt sorry for those who could not.

One of my classmates loved to sing, but he always sang off key. It bothered my ears, but I never said anything to him. I didn't understand why he couldn't hear that he was flat or sharp.

Relative pitch came to me naturally, which made it hard for me to realize that everyone else wasn't so fortunate.

Junior and senior high school. While I was in junior high, high school music instructor Don Gunderson asked three of us to sing with his choir. I suppose our junior high music teacher recommended us, or maybe Mr. Gunderson was desperate for voices. Anyway, my two classmates and I trooped across the road to the high school once a day for his vocal music class—a "big deal" to us. My sisters Westella and Erdyne were high school students at the time and probably weren't too thrilled to have their little brother in choir with them.

Mr. Gunderson always said that he didn't know where to put me. I could hit high C along with the sopranos, but the girls didn't want a boy singing soprano. I could

also sing tenor, but the high school tenors weren't thrilled to have this scrawny junior high kid in their midst. Choir members accepted me as I rotated from soprano to tenor because Mr. Gunderson was the boss.

As such, he never hesitated to respond when I misbehaved. Once he threw me out when I was innocent. As a prank, a bass standing right behind me snipped my ear with his fingernail clipper during the middle of a song. He only nicked it, but it felt like he had amputated my entire ear. I grabbed my ear and shrieked in pain, disrupting the rehearsal. Mr. Gunderson's head jerked up, he stopped the choir, and without saying a word, he pointed to the door. That was worse than having him yell at me.

"Someone nicked my ear!" I protested.

The entire row of basses looked so innocent. No one admitted guilt. For once I was not the instigator, but I had to leave the rehearsal. Later the offender confessed to me privately that it was he who nicked my ear.

Admittedly, I was not always the innocent victim. I never did anything bad, but sometimes I was the one who started it all. I liked to make others laugh, and rehearsals became prime time for me. I walked my fingers on the shoulders of students standing in front of me.

In the early 1950s, Bill Riley brought his Iowa State Fair Talent Search to small towns in Iowa, including Centerville. I won first prize singing "Sweet Little Jesus Boy" in the same auditorium which was later named in my honor. More than 40 years later, in 1996, I was the guest soloist for Bill Riley's[3] farewell concert at the stage named for him at the Iowa State Fair.

V.1234

Sweet Little Jesus Boy

Words and Music by
ROBERT Mac GIMSEY

Sing this song with the simplicity of a lullaby to a child.
Never hurry the words. Dwell on the meaningful words here
and there according to your own feelings, and maintain no
rhythm whatsoever.
Bear in mind that this is a meditative song of suppressed emo-
...ung by you intimately to the Jesus Child.

When they jumped in surprise, I quickly withdrew my hand. As my victim whirled around to confront me, I maintained eye contact with Mr. Gunderson and looked as innocent as I could. Sometimes it worked and sometimes the voice of Mr. Gunderson quickly put an end to my antics. "Estes—out!" he would thunder as he pointed to the door.

Special Songs. My special solos were "Sweet Little Jesus Boy" and "On Top of Old Smoky" which I sang an octave higher in the soprano range. I wasn't very tall and I was so skinny. My choir robe looked as if I could run laps inside it and not disturb a single fold.

After one of my concert solos, I noticed Jim Poffenberger's mother crying. I felt terrible and wondered what made her so sad. After the performance, Mrs. Poffenberger came up to me and said she had been moved to tears by my beautiful singing. Every so often I still notice people in the audience with tears in their eyes. To me, that compliment far surpasses applause.

Being Judged. I often sang "Sweet Little Jesus Boy" in music contests but never earned a top rating. After one particular contest, two of my friends told my mother that my performance deserved a first place but, in their opinion, the judges were prejudiced. Don Gunderson agreed. I received second or third place, while white competitors always won first place.

Don was furious with the judges because they paid more attention to white students. When my turn came to sing, Don watched the judges continue to write about the previous contestant or leave the room to have a smoke. After I sang, they scribbled a few lines and waited for the next student. This injustice made Don boil with anger. The lower rankings disappointed me, and I hoped only for the same consideration the white students received. I wanted to be judged on my voice—not my color.

Kindly Actions. Many years later, Don Gunderson told me a story about going to the All-State Chorus. Every Thanksgiving weekend, the best high school voices in Iowa gathered in Des Moines to rehearse for a Saturday night concert. Several members of our choir, including me, were invited to sing with the All-Staters in Des Moines, some 90 miles from Centerville. (Ames, Iowa, now hosts the concert.)

We stayed in hotels for several nights while away from home. It never occurred to me that sleeping arrangements presented a problem. Many times I spent the night in the homes of my white friends in Centerville and never thought some choir members would object to sharing a room with me in Des Moines.

When the boys paired off for rooms, I learned I would room with Mr. Gunderson. The surprise made me feel so special. Little did I know he was the only person willing to share a room with a black. That's just one of the reasons I respected Mr. Gunderson so much.

Hidden talents. Mario Lanza, the well-known tenor, was at the peak of his career when I was in high school. I liked his choice of music, and I had some of his old 78 rpm records from which I learned to imitate his "operatic" voice.

At home, my Lanza impersonation rattled the windows, but I never sang like that outside the house. For some reason, I was afraid to tell Don Gunderson that I imitated Lanza.

One day as my sister Erdyne and I talked, I mentioned my reluctance to tell Mr. Gunderson about my Lanza technique. Taking matters into her own hands, she approached him: "My brother can sing in a different style. Would you like to hear that?"

Out of curiosity, he agreed to set a time and date. With trepidation, I tilted my head back and let loose with my version of "Granada." I sang in Spanish because I learned it that way from the record. He stared at me in amazement. He said he couldn't believe how well I imitated Mario Lanza and how well I sang in Spanish.

Voice changes. Fortunately, my soprano voice didn't last and Mario Lanza's career was safe. But it wasn't until my senior year in high school that my voice changed. No longer did I challenge the sopranos because my high C disappeared. Not only was my voice changing, but it seemed to be disappearing.

Mr. Gunderson sent me to a throat doctor who said there was nothing physically wrong with my voice — it was just developing. I did not sing well for months because my range consisted of about four notes.

This influenced my decision in choosing a college major. Vocal music seemed to be out of the question and medicine seemed a much better choice. At this point, conversation suited my voice better than singing.

Moving On

After a year at Centerville Junior College (now a campus of Indian Hills Community College), I was ready to leave home for a new environment at the State University of Iowa in Iowa City (now the University of Iowa). While leaving behind all I knew, my immediate problem was money since my parents could not afford to pay my college expenses. I had no idea what would happen, but I was optimistic.

From 1957 to 1960, I experienced some of the happiest days of my life. In the nurturing academic atmosphere of the University of Iowa, I felt a freedom I had never known. Many of the restrictions I had faced because of color diminished considerably. I met people with whom I could share ideas, dreams, and aspirations.

More important, my peers accepted me as a person. Not until I married and had children did my happiness surpass that of those University days. As the years went by, I switched from medicine to religion to psychology and finally to music. Choosing a major was a difficult decision.

Financially, Iowa City was never an easy time for me. When I reflect on those days, I remember the problems and pain of not having money. There were many hungry days and many nights when I slept on the floor.

Nothing would have made my father happier than to help pay for my education. Despite his own limited background, he valued education highly and encouraged me to continue with mine. This man who could only sign his name

MADRIGAL GROUP - 1954
Division I State Contest
L to R,Roger White, Simon
Estes, Judi Johnston, June
Guffey, Jean Stewart, Nancy
Plowman, Judy Dooley, Nancy
Hendershot, Bill Milani, Bill
Simmons

MIXED QUARTET - 1956
L to R, Judy Broshar,Accomp.
Simon Estes,Mary Ellen Clarke,
Mary Powers,Bob Auld

singing in senior High School

and read a few words wanted me to have a better life. He saw education as the way to that life and tried to help me by borrowing $500 with our family home as collateral.

Dressed in his Sunday suit, he walked to the town square. Centerville had three banks and he approached all three. His house was worth twice the $500 he wanted to borrow. He knew it was a large sum, but he also knew he could repay the debt with the same hard work that sustained our family up to that point.

One after another, all three banks turned him down. My father knew better than to argue with the white bankers. He left each one with a polite "thank you."

Undaunted, he came up with another idea and asked his brother Oakey to put up his house as collateral, too. Uncle Oakey agreed, and once again my father made his rounds to the banks with *two* houses as collateral. The answer from all three banks remained the same. "No."

The banks' refusals distressed my father. He could only assume his color barred him from the loan. As a result, my father was unable to help me with expenses, although there was nothing else he wanted more in the world.

Making Money. To earn a little extra money, Jim Galloway and I joined the National Guard in 1958. We were the 1950s version of Willie and Joe, Bill Mauldin's foxhole jockeys. Jim and I were no doubt the two sorriest soldiers who ever attended summer camp in Minnesota.

When it became known that I was supporting my mother and brother, I received an early discharge. In 1994, almost 40 years later, the Iowa National Guard made me an Honorary Colonel.

They allowed me to fly in an F-16 fighter jet and even trusted me to drive an M-1A Abrams tank.

Throughout my college years, I worked a variety of jobs. Some were in construction, several were in restaurants where I could earn a little money and a meal, and some were in the janitorial line like at the Iowa City *Press Citizen*. I worked there from 12:30 AM until 5:30 AM and then attended classes during the day. I also worked for Collins Radio in Cedar Rapids. I started on the assembly line and worked my way up to expediter, where I made sure everyone had the needed parts.

I held various jobs on campus, as well. One of the first jobs was in the cafeteria for the Quadrangle Dormitory. Soon after I began working there, I noticed that only white students served food and punched meal cards, while the black students washed dishes. Once when my boss was in the kitchen, I asked her if the division of workers amounted to discrimination. The lady was indignant at my question.

"Absolutely not," she snapped. "We assign jobs in the order they are applied for and all the dining room jobs were taken when the blacks applied."

I shook my head and politely told her that I could not accept that explanation.

"Well," she insisted, "it's true. Besides, students don't want their food served by blacks."

I replied, "College students are so hungry, they don't care who serves them."

"I suppose," she accused, raising an eyebrow at me, "you want one of those jobs yourself."

"No," I told her. "This is not a personal issue but a discrimination issue. I will stay in the

Jim Galloway and I join the Iowa National Guard.

kitchen washing pots and pans, but I want to see a black student in a more prestigious position. This is important to me and I might bring it up at the next student council meeting."

I didn't want to threaten her, but this truly mattered to me.

Annoyed, she answered, "Okay, I will do it, but if he doesn't work out, it's your fault."

"No," I quickly responded, "if you hire a black student, you are just hiring a human being who can make mistakes as easily as any other human being. It's up to you to hire a responsible person. Then, if that person fails, you cannot persecute all black workers. You'll just have to find another one better suited to the job."

At that moment, my boss was livid but, after thinking it over, she hired a black student to serve in the dining room. When it didn't work out, she fired him and came straight to me.

I gave her the name of another black student and, with his hiring, her problems were over.

Later, to her credit she was responsible for hiring the first black person to serve in the Quad's restaurant on a permanent basis.

Food. Money was always a terrible problem. So was food—or the lack of it. As a growing young man, my body constantly required nourishment in large quantities, but I learned to survive on far less than I care to remember. At one time, I existed on a handful of cereal and water for breakfast.

The Jefferson Hotel offered a special of blueberry pancakes, three sausages, and a glass of milk for 87 cents. That became my main meal

"King for a Day"

which had to last 24 hours. By dining at four, I could study at night and not be hungry, eat some cereal for "brunch," and make it until four the next afternoon without too many hunger pains.

Eventually, the financial burden became too much and I dropped out of the University for a semester.

Residence Life. That semester I had a problem with a dorm—or maybe they had a problem with me. Because of my financial difficulties, I didn't enroll in classes, but some of my buddies let me stay in their dorm rooms. I had a campus job and sang with the Old Gold Singers, acting as if I were a full-time student. I assumed no one would find me out.

Then it happened. Dorm residents elected me their "King." I even attended a dance with a young lady who seemed to be impressed with her royal date. However, my reign as king was a short one. The next day the authorities

dethroned and "de-dormatized" me. It seemed that the laws of the kingdom required a tuition-paying king. Reluctantly, I relinquished my crown and moved out of the dorm.

The authorities were good sports about the entire incident. So were my friends who had jeopardized their status as University students by harboring a pretender to the throne. I refer to that period in my life as the "King for a Day" adventure.

Conflict. I soon learned that Iowa City was much more the "big city" than Centerville. One evening I borrowed a car from a friend to take my date to a movie. After I dropped her off at her dorm, I returned the car and started walking home. As I headed down Iowa Avenue, three white guys stopped me right in front of Joe's Bar, one of the college hangouts. One sized me up and said, "Hello, Spider," referring to my tall, skinny appearance.

I should have walked around them and ignored the comment, but I stopped and innocently asked, "Why did you call me 'Spider'?"

The same man snarled at me, "Because I wanted to call you 'Spider.'"

Still trying to be pleasant, I responded, "If you asked my name, I would tell you and you wouldn't have to call me 'Spider.'" I wasn't in any way antagonizing, but I wanted them to know I didn't appreciate being called names.

One of his friends leaned toward me and hit me so hard that I spun around and found myself facing the door to Joe's. Trying to maintain my balance, I ran inside.

The bartender looked up as I sprinted toward him. One eye was swelling shut.

"What happened to you?" he asked with concern. I explained the incident and as I finished, the same three men who harassed me walked in the front door.

Despite the presence of the bartender and customers, I still didn't feel safe.

One of the men approached me. It was not the man who hit me, but I still didn't want anything to do with him. He stopped a few feet away and said in a low voice, "I'm sorry for what my friend did. He had no right to hit you. I'm very, very sorry." With that, the three men turned and left the bar.

The next day I went to work looking a bit battered around the face. My fellow students wanted to know what had happened. They were upset when I told the story. Several of the athletic types wanted to seek revenge. Although I appreciated their concern, I told them, "No. More violence will not solve anything."

"Come on Si," one of them urged. "Who are they? We'll wipe them out."

I stuck to my guns and didn't tell. Any recriminations by my friends could have caused a totally unnecessary racial incident. I was thankful one of the other men apologized and knew that further violence would solve nothing.

Dating. My first Iowa City date was with a lovely black girl. I'd invited her to a formal campus dance and, to my amazement, she agreed. I thought she was the most beautiful girl in the world. How exciting to think she would attend this dance with me! By the evening of the dance, I was a bundle of nerves. Since I didn't have a suit, I wore my ROTC uniform and borrowed a car from a friend. We double-dated with another black couple.

When the dance ended, we took the girls back to their dorm. In those days, the girls had to be back by midnight, so I kept a careful eye on my watch. My dating experience may have been minimal, but I knew how to be a gentleman.

As I walked my date to the door of her dorm, I noticed the other couple locked in a passionate embrace and assumed they were dating steadily. On the first time out with my date, I knew I shouldn't try to kiss her. That was just how a gentleman treated a lady.

When we reached the door, I shook her hand and said, "I've really enjoyed this evening and I'd like to see you again." She smiled, said she'd had a good time too, and went inside.

I floated back to my room. My roommate waited up for me. He noticed the grin on my face and said, "Hey Roomie, how was the date?"

"Great," I told him.

The "lighter" music group—The Old Gold Singers

He asked if we had done more than shake hands at the door. That upset me and I wondered, "How could you say anything like that? It was our *first* date!"

He then proceeded to question me further using popular black lingo I'd never learned in Centerville. I knew what he was talking about because I'd heard those phrases on campus. I was furious. "She is a fine lady and I don't like the way you are talking about her."

"Come on. You mean to tell me you didn't even kiss her?"

"No, I just shook her hand."

He exploded with laughter. From then on, he called me "Shake-a-hand Si." As I got ready to turn in, he told me that the young lady I'd just been out with had a bad reputation.

That really upset me. She was my first love and I defended her honor. "Please," I said in a stilted voice, "don't talk about her that way."

My roommate chuckled, "It's late. Go to bed and get some sleep." I asked that young lady out again, but she always turned me down.

Black and Gold. Despite my forays into psychology, religion, and medicine, music reappeared with the same regularity as spring. I auditioned for the large University of Iowa chorus composed of some 230 voices. When the director rejected me, he said my voice was not good enough.

As an alternative, he suggested, "There is a group on campus where your voice might be better suited. Their repertoire consists of lighter music which they perform at conventions, dinners, and our Varsity Varieties." My voice wasn't good enough to blend with 230 others but would be acceptable with 23?

The "lighter" music group to which he referred was the Old Gold Singers founded in 1958. Undaunted by his remarks, I contacted Jerry Lawson, director of this group, and auditioned for him. I appreciated his honesty when he told me that he liked my voice, but before he could say yes, he would have to ask the other students if they objected to having a black person in the group. Their only question was: "Can he sing?" to which Jerry Lawson replied, "He has a beautiful voice." I became a member of the Old Gold Singers.

The school colors were black and gold, hence the name Old Gold Singers. With me in the group they could become the "Old Black and Gold Singers" if they so chose! I made some very good friends among this congenial group. I was proud to be part of them.

Charles Kellis. When a new faculty person joins a department, he or she often is tossed a few crusts of bread and many crumbs in the way of students. Charles Kellis, who joined the music department at Iowa in 1961, was no exception. According to the music department, I was in the crumb category. I know that someone up there watched over me because Mr. Kellis became my wonderful mentor and opened a whole new world to me.

An Iowa staff member told him I had no voice and it would be a waste of time if he accepted me as a student. Mr. Kellis paid no attention to this warning and added me to his roster. His first impression of me was a "skinny, sweet, under-nourished kid with a remarkable voice." From the beginning, he felt in his heart I had a voice worthy of his time and talent, and I liked him from our first meeting.

Mr. Kellis loaned me recordings by Enrico Caruso, Leontyne Price, Eileen Farrell, and Cesare Siepi.

I said to him the next day, "You know what? I really like that stuff!"

My mentor and friend, Mr. Charles Kellis

However, there was a problem. I worked at Collins to support my mother and brother and money was tight. I had no way to pay him for lessons, but because he believed in me, Mr. Kellis gave me daily four- to five-hour lessons at no cost. He taught me not only about opera but also about kindness and sharing.

When I couldn't afford to pay him for lessons, I said, "Mr. Kellis, one of these days when I have money, I will repay you for all these lessons and your time."

He replied, "Simon, I know you will become successful in your singing career and when you do, my pay will be that you remain humble."

I have never forgotten those words; I hope I repay him the way he wanted.

Mr. Kellis told me later that other faculty members questioned him about the time he "wasted" on Estes but, luckily for me, he ignored their criticism. Little did they realize what the team of Kellis and Estes would achieve!

Charles Kellis and I developed a mutual admiration all our own which has never involved control of my private life. He is my best friend and remains my voice teacher. I believe that God sent Charles Kellis to discover, teach, coach, and direct the operatic voice I have. This one man had faith that I could sing opera.

New York, New York. In 1962, I began preparing for my audition at The Juilliard School of Music in New York City. Mr. Kellis and Fred Dewhart, my roommate, asked permission for me to charge admission to one of my concerts in order to earn money for the trip.

University of Iowa President Hancher himself granted permission, and I gave that concert in the Methodist Church on Dubuque Street in Iowa City.

In 1963, Mr. Kellis arranged an audition for me at The Juilliard School. In addition to my fund-raising concert, I worked that spring and summer to earn money for the trip to New York. What an incentive! Now my life would move from Iowa to New York.

My decision to study music at The Juilliard School shocked my mother. "What's opera?" She responded with the very same question I had asked Mr. Kellis when he first recommended opera to me! I couldn't give her a very good answer at that time, but I told her an opera performer sings quite loudly in a foreign language.

I explained, "Mr. Kellis is trying to arrange an audition at The Juilliard School of Music in New York. He thinks I have a good chance of getting a scholarship. He'll help me find work and a place to live."

"Why would you give up your good job at Collins Radio, move to New York, and try to make your living singing opera?" my mother worried. According to her music philosophy, singing is for the Lord. He gave me this voice, so I should use it to sing for Him in churches. How could I go from helping people with my studies in medicine to entertaining them with opera music?

"Mother," I insisted, "I feel I should go. Mr. Kellis said my voice is suited for this type of music. I want to try it.

"You know, Mother, in a way I will still be a doctor. I may not be treating someone's physical ailment, but through music, I can bring joy to people. It's a beautiful form of entertainment, so I am doing something for their souls, for their minds, and for their hearts. Music is a form of medicine that heals the ills all people carry. If I can be a part of that, my life will be worthwhile."

She was convinced by my arguments. "Son," she said, "if you really believe in this, you've got my blessing."

The audition. I took my first commercial flight ever to New York several days ahead of my audition. I didn't want to risk arriving late.

"Simon, you shouldn't have flown and spent all that money," Mr. Kellis scolded when I landed. "I would have set a different time for you at The Juilliard School so you wouldn't be late and you could have saved the $200 airfare." He knew how closely I watched my pennies. I appreciated his concern, but it didn't matter at that point. I was in New York and ready for new adventures!

In preparation for my audition, I received several lessons from Mr. Kellis. As I entered The Juilliard School, I felt the resonating presence of musical history. I didn't know much about Mozart, Beethoven, Brahms, or Schubert, but I knew this was a very, very special place. I even liked the smell of the building.

I began with King Philip's aria from *Don Carlo*. The jury sat stoically as I sang. Would I make it? I sang to make Mr. Kellis proud.

To my amazement, I was not only accepted, but I also received both a grant from the Martha Baird Rockefeller Foundation and a full academic scholarship. Everything was falling into place.

Job hungry. Now I needed a job because I had to pay my bills as well as those of my mother and brother who moved from Iowa City to Des Moines to live with my aunt, Hazel Powell. Luckily, I found jobs in the school cafeteria and at the Lincoln Center leading tours.

I was fortunate to find an apartment anywhere near The Juilliard School. I hated to leave the

The Juilliard School of Music in New York City

YMCA because it was so inexpensive, but a writer named Gordon Rogoff rented me a great room on West 96th.

The kid from Centerville was about to enter a life he'd never even dreamed about. The strong foundation of faith, love, education, and endurance established by my parents would serve me well.

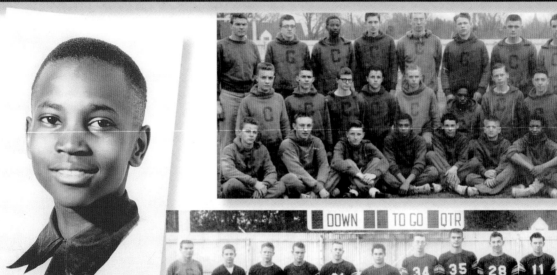

Centerville High school days—chorus, track, and football

CENTERVILLE H.S.
Big Reds
CENTERVILLE, IOWA

My older sister Erdyne had strict orders from Mother to walk me home on extremely windy days.

My mother, Ruth Jeter, shown here on the right, grew up poor in Centerville. Her mother gave birth to ten children and died at an early age, leaving "Papa" to raise the children by himself. Hazel, shown on the left, had to leave school to help with the younger children.

The east side of the Centerville town square

My family is more important to me than any career or social life could ever be. I'd rather spend my time at home with my girls than anywhere else in the world.

Whether in the concert hall or in church, my mother and sisters have always been there for me. In 1997, Mother, Erdyne, and I visited the little house at 910 East Jackson in Centerville, where I spent the early years of my life.

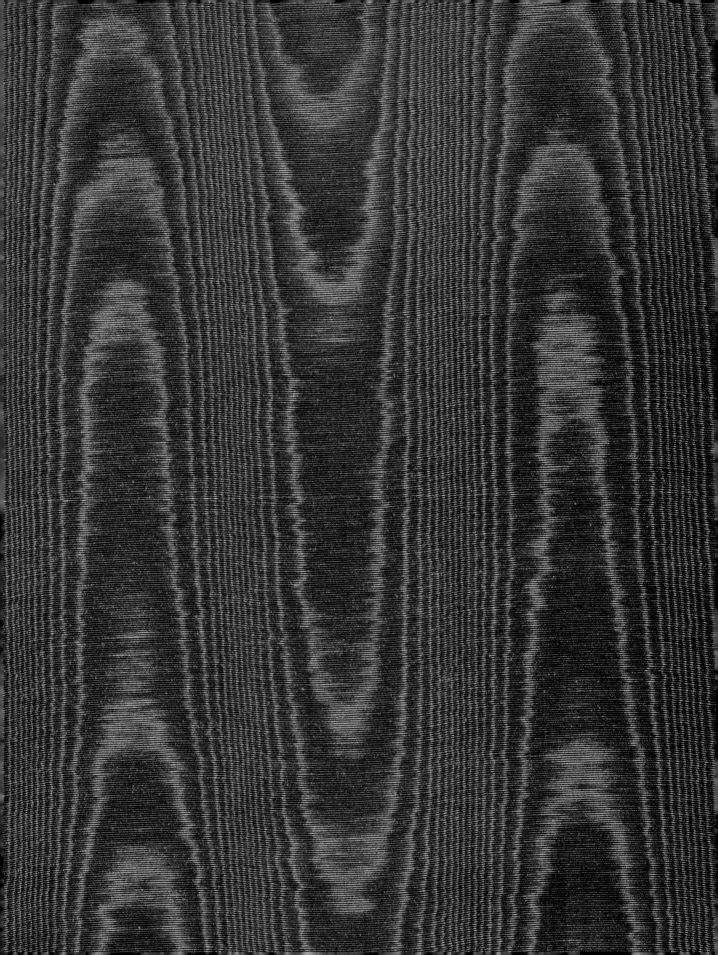

CHAPTER TWO

The Music

I studied at The Juilliard School for a year, getting training in theory, musicianship, and sight reading. During my limited time there, I received just a smattering of what is offered at The Juilliard School during the typical five-year degree program or the six- or seven-year master's degree program. Being able to sing with some of the finest conductors also provided excellent learning experiences.

While at The Juilliard School, I enjoyed spending time with Pauline, a fellow student and singer. Before long, she was eager to start her career and left for Germany. I missed her, and as Christmas approached, I decided to spend the holidays with her. As usual, my biggest problem came in finding the money. We devised a plan. If Pauline found auditions for me in

Germany, then I could go to Europe, too. Through an agent, Pauline arranged an audition with the Deutsche Oper, West Berlin's main opera house.

But how could I pay for a plane ticket? I approached several organizations for grant money. The NAACP (National Association for the Advancement of Colored People) didn't have a fund for aspiring singers, but the office staff liked me and took up their own collection of $267. I also received $1000 from the New York Community Trust Fund and a grant from the Martha Baird Rockefeller Foundation, so I set off for Berlin, Christmas with Pauline, and the Deutsche Oper.

My audition went extremely well. My voice impressed the intendant (director of music) and he offered me a role as the King of Egypt in their

The Kid from Centerville was about to enter a life he'd never even dreamed about.

spring production of Verdi's *Aida*. I was ecstatic because landing a role with the Deutsche Oper compared to starting at the Metropolitan Opera House in New York City.

A new friend. I went along for support when Pauline sang in a competition. While waiting for the activities to begin, I noticed another black man and introduced myself. Julius Tilghman had come from Baltimore to accompany a young black singer whom he knew from college. I told him to start packing because Pauline would win this competition hands down. In a lofty voice, Julius informed me that his singer would wipe mine off the face of the earth, no doubt about it.

The competition began. When Julius's singer sang her first notes, I knew Pauline was in big trouble. Jessye Norman's incredible voice diminished that of everyone else.

Julius remains a good friend and excellent accompanist. Since we first met, he has traveled with me all over Europe and the United States. His humor always entertains me, and his rich philosophical discussions keep my mind in tune.

German adventure. Pauline continued auditioning, but any singing roles eluded her. It was January, and my rehearsals didn't begin until April, so we decided to travel around Germany.

Then I did a stupid thing: I exchanged my return airline ticket for travel money. Pauline wisely kept hers.

When we arrived in Dusseldorf after traveling throughout the country, we had nearly depleted our funds. Reality finally dawned on me: I had neither money to stay in Germany nor a return plane ticket so I could leave.

There was only one thing to do. I called "Mr. Fixit"—Charles Kellis. He was incredulous. "You did what?" he sputtered. "You turned in your return ticket and toured Germany? Simon, why did you do such a stupid thing?"

"It seemed like a good idea at the time," I said, embarrassed. I could have added that we really enjoyed ourselves, but I knew that was inappropriate. Instead, I asked how I could earn money to pay for my trip home.

Mr. Kellis suggested I contact the American Embassy. Was there an American cruise ship sailing on which I could sing for my passage home? No such luck.

We reasoned that since Pauline had been smart enough to keep her ticket, she should fly home and find money for me to pay the hotel bill and buy another return ticket. On her flight back to the States, Pauline sat next to a man who gave her $60 upon hearing of my sad story. She must have altered the real story, because no one with good sense would have given me a dime. As soon as she landed at JFK airport, she wired the money to me. The next day, a mutual friend gave her enough money for my return fare.

The Debut

While I was back in the United States, I worked long and hard with Mr. Kellis on the King of Egypt role for my debut. Upon my arrival at the Deutsche Oper, the gentleman who had hired me announced, "Oh, by the way Simon, we changed your role. You will now be singing the part of Ramfis, the high priest." This was a much bigger role than the King of Egypt.

"But I learned the King of Egypt role!" I protested. I couldn't believe what I heard.

"Ah, you Americans!" He laughed and waved his hands. "You all learn music so fast. It will be no problem for you."

Was this a test or a cruel joke? Surely they didn't expect me to learn a brand new role in 13 days? Once again I turned to Charles Kellis. Like me, he was very upset. "Simon, I've never heard of giving a role to a beginner to learn in 13 days, but I know you can do it. Get a coach from the opera house, borrow the records, listen to the part, and work on it day and night."

I made my debut in Germany on April 19, 1965. Thanks to the makeup people, I was as white as a ghost. Throughout the years, white people have put on black makeup, but few blacks did the reverse. However, for this performance I was made up in white face. Not just white, but white white. I looked six shades lighter than any other performer. When I looked in the mirror, I was embarrassed. While I examined my ghost-like face, the makeup people pulled a rubber cap over my hair so I looked bald. Why the audience didn't go into convulsive laughter when I made my entrance, I'll never know.

This debut was fraught with firsts. I performed my first major role in a major opera, a role I learned in 13 days. It marked my first time on the main stage since we had only used the prac-

tice stage in rehearsals, and the first time I had a white face and a bald head. I met the conductor for the first time when I walked on stage and began to sing. No one told him the high priest was a rank amateur. As he raised his baton, he smiled at me, confident that a seasoned American singer was under his direction. In retrospect, all of these things except the white face and bald head should have terrified me, but that night I felt rather calm and the opera was a huge success. I sang that role for ten months and gained much-needed stage experience.

A crossroads. During the early stages of my career, an opera house administrator called me to his office. He motioned for us to sit. "I enjoyed your performance, Mr. Estes. Your singing was wonderful. Your voice is beautiful."

He took off his glasses and looked directly into my eyes. "I am a very important man in this country. I have contacts with recording companies and other opera houses. You are very handsome. I can do much for you and your career."

The word "handsome" tipped me off and I knew exactly what he implied. I had to extricate myself from this conversation without offending him. This man could probably make or break my career, but I would never compromise my principles. I sat up straighter and took a deep breath. "Thank you very much. I am interested only in getting experience on the stage musically and dramatically." I watched to see if he understood my message, but I couldn't tell.

Without a trace of emotion, he replied, "Of course, Mr. Estes, that's why I engaged you. I do want you to remember if there is anything else [and he emphasized *anything*] I can do for you, I am always here. Please don't hesitate to contact me." He ended the conversation with a smile, but it seemed more of a leer. I could tell he thought, "You will be back, Mr. Estes."

I confided my suspicions to a friend who was a very famous singer with the opera house. She asked about my salary and couldn't believe I received a monthly salary equivalent to $500 in American money—a large sum for that time and unheard of for a beginner. She felt the director thought I would acquiesce to his demands in order to keep my salary at that level.

The opera company signed me up for another role. My original contract extended for two years, but now it read "for one role at a time." Soon the director called me to his office. "We can't afford to pay you [$500] a month," he told me. "We can only afford to pay you [$375]."

"That's fine. I can live on that," I answered, and easily could since I was single with few expenses.

He called me in a third time and notified me that my salary was cut to $250 a month. Not only did my pay diminish, but so did the number of singing roles I received. Finally, they paid me per role and the money dwindled to a mere pittance as the roles became smaller.

Now I struggled to make ends meet. I lived in a rooming house owned by a delightful and kind older lady. As my situation worsened, I confided in her. She told me she admired my principles and encouraged me to be strong and not give in to the director's subtle demands. The day came when I could not pay for my room. "Mr. Estes," she said with a kind smile, "you may stay here as long as you wish. When your salary is better, you can pay me. But for now, don't worry."

I felt terrible because she relied on this money to support herself, and I vowed to repay every penny. That woman's kindness gave me strength. She knew that if I couldn't pay my rent, I couldn't pay for food. She made liverwurst sandwiches for me, and many days these sandwiches and water sustained me. I will never forget this lovely, kind, principled lady who had faith in me and helped me in such troubled times. I repaid her in full some years later.

The Munich Competition. In 1965 while in Germany, I won third place in the Munich competition, one of the most respected competitions in the opera world. This win opened opera house doors throughout Germany for me. It also served as a warm-up for other challenges.

The Tchaikovsky Competition. The Institute of International Education asked me, an American, to enter the Tchaikovsky Competition in Moscow. This prestigious event traditionally turns the international spotlight to young musicians and virtually guarantees their success. Probably the most famous American winner of this competition is Van Cliburn, the pianist. As my sponsor, the Institute would pay my way to Moscow. The Russians would then pay expenses during my stay, provide an accompanist, and pay for a return ticket. If by some fluke I won, I would receive a monetary stipend in rubles.

The Tchaikovsky Competition required participants to sing a number of songs in Russian. "I'll do it," I said with great confidence, "but there is one problem. I don't know Russian."

"Don't worry," came the Institute's reply. "We'll send you money for lessons." The money never came.

My contract with the opera house at which I was performing presented another obstacle. I asked the director to release me for the Tchaikovsky competition. "No problem," came the answer, but when the time arrived for my trip, he decided I couldn't go.

"If you do, you'll be fired," the director announced. "I advise you not to leave the city. If you choose to disobey, I will see that you don't sing in Germany again."

Being young and inexperienced, I was in a quandary. I promised the Institute I'd go to Moscow, but feared leaving Germany and risking my career there. I had auditioned for the Hamburg opera which hired me to sing in the world premiere of Gunter Schuller's opera *The Visitation* and didn't want to lose that upcoming opportunity. After several days of worrying, I told a friend about my conversation with the director.

"Don't listen to him," my friend advised. "Get on the train, go see the manager of the Hamburg Opera, and discuss the situation with him." I bought a ticket for Hamburg and boarded the train. I felt very nervous. Mr. Lieberman, the Hamburg director, listened to my story and then said, "Simon, I would still engage you to sing here. Don't worry about it."

I had prayed about this conflict and now I saw it resolved. For the next step I prayed: "God, I'm not asking you to grant great favors. Please just bring about what you think is right."

Reassured, I boarded the flight from East Germany to Moscow. On this long flight, I sat next to a Russian actress who also spoke German. During our conversation, I told her about the competition. I showed her the music and asked if she had heard of any of the pieces.

This dear lady looked over the musical scores and selected her favorite: "Ni Slova, O Drug Moi" which means "Not a Word, Oh My Friend." During the flight, she taught me the lyrics phonetically. Once I arrived in Moscow, I attended a

Not knowing a word of Russian, I boarded the plane for Moscow and the Tchaikovsky Competition with only my music and my faith in God.

practice session with my accompanist, a Russian woman named Irena Zorina. She listened to my first song and tactfully said, "Your Russian is not so good, but we will work on it."

We did, and our work paid off—I won the first round. *Pravda*, the Russian newspaper, said my Russian was better than any of my competitors'. Fortunately, my short slow song made it much easier. My success in the first round meant advancement to the second round. Now I had to sing *four* songs in Russian from memory.

Irena Zorina was very proud of our success, especially since I came so unprepared. She couldn't believe that I entered this important competition without knowing the Russian language or any Russian songs. At first she thought it pointless to continue, but then changed her mind and said, "We must try!" We worked four days and nights with very little time off, and somehow I learned all the songs.

My performance included an aria from *Eugene Onégin*, a song as well known by

Russians as "Ol' Man River" is by Americans. Halfway through this aria, out of the corner of my eye, I noticed a flurry of activity as Irena turned pages in a mad scramble. I knew in an instant what I had done. I had skipped the middle section and had sung only the beginning and the end. The sound of 2000 people in the audience going "Uhhhhhhhh" like a hurricane let me know I had just bought my ticket home.

I lifted my chest and sang on as if nothing had happened. After that disaster, I sang the next three songs without a single mistake.

The judging panel consisted of Russians, Eastern Europeans, and an American, George London. George later told me the judges thought my voice was beautiful, and they advanced me to the next round because I handled my mistake so well. They were impressed when I finished that bungled aria and made it through the other pieces. George also said I would have won first prize if I hadn't made that mistake. Instead I won third.

My winnings included the bronze medal and I received the third prize money in rubles. I could only bring out one-fourth of the money in American currency, so I bought a few souvenirs and a watch for my mother. The rest remained in a Russian savings account.

Since I couldn't take the rubles out, I thought I would be clever and buy a round-trip plane ticket for later use. The ticket proved to be worthless because rubles weren't honored in the Western world.

However, winning in the Competition was invaluable for advancing my professional career. Even though I only won third prize it was enough to bring my name to the attention of people in the United States.

My Tchaikovsky Competition winnings included a bronze medal and prize money in rubles.

Dinner at the White House. President Lyndon Johnson invited all the American winners of the Tchaikovsky Competition to dinner at the White House, including Veronica Tyler, Jane Marsh, Misha Dichter, and Stephen Kates. One of the greatest joys of the evening was sharing it with my mother.

The taste of success. Another perk from the competition was the opportunity to sing in such places as the Hollywood Bowl. While having breakfast at the Hollywood Roosevelt Hotel on my first trip to California, I heard my name over the public address system.

Mr. Simon Estes will please present this card at THE SOUTHWEST GATE The White House Thursday, November 21, 1968 at 6:00 o'clock NOT TRANSFERABLE

The President and Mrs. Johnson request the pleasure of the company of Mr. Estes at a reception to be held at The White House on Thursday evening, November 21, 1968 at six o'clock

SIMON ESTES
Bass-baritone

"Simon Estes, you have a phone call at the front desk." Despite the simplicity of that message, I felt like the most important person in the world, called to the phone just like a movie star or an important executive. Here I was, the kid from Centerville, Iowa, staying in Hollywood like the movie stars, singing in the Hollywood Bowl, and being paged. I can't remember who called, but I will never forget that wonderful feeling as I walked across the floor to the phone.

My only disappointment related to the Competition was that the Metropolitan Opera didn't contact me even for a beginner's contract, the first step in a relationship with the Met. It would have entitled me to lessons, small roles in productions, and most importantly, experience.

Career Crescendos

In 1966, Columbia Artists Management Incorporated (CAMI) sought to add a bass baritone to its roster. After one of their representatives mentioned this to Veronica Tyler, a friend and an excellent singer herself, I auditioned, and received a contract the same day.

Due to the efforts of Michael Ries, my CAMI manager, my career escalated in America as well as in Europe. I persistently asked for more work, and he found places for me to sing like no agent since. In our first year alone, I sang in 45 recitals. I performed at Tanglewood with the Boston Symphony, at the Hollywood Bowl, on the "Tonight Show" with Johnny Carson, and with the Philadelphia Orchestra, to name a few. I loved singing in the United States! Those years are some of my career favorites because I met and mingled with people who are the heart of America.

Michael believed in my voice and he believed in me. We shared ideas and we listened to each other, all for the advancement of my career.

Unforgettable experiences. Many wonderful experiences highlight my career. One special event occurred in 1972, when I had the honor of singing at the Opening Ceremonies of the Olympic Games in Munich. Another took place when the Concert Hall at the Kennedy Center opened in 1973 in Washington, D.C., and violinist Isaac Stern and I were chosen to participate in dedicating this magnificent hall. We met President Nixon and his family. What an honor to sing for this opening!

In 1982, I had the great distinction of being the first African-American man to open the season at New York City's Metropolitan Opera. I sang the role of Landgraf in Wagner's *Tannhäuser.*

In 1986, I performed in New York with the Boston Pops Orchestra at the Statue of Liberty Centennial Celebration. Later, I sang in New Jersey at the Meadowlands with Whitney Houston, Barry Manilow, Johnny Cash, and others.

I performed twice for President George Bush and Mrs. Bush. The first event in 1989 was a televised program called "In Performance at the White House" with several other artists and John Denver as host.

The second time, the Bushes were entertaining Corazón Aquino, President of the Philippines, and I was the solo performer. To be invited back by these gracious people was very gratifying.

A high point in my career was singing for Nelson Mandela at the Riverside Baptist Church in New York. He spoke about what needed to be done, not what had happened to him. Even though he had been incarcerated for half of his life, he expressed no bitterness or anger. To be in the presence of this man was a very humbling experience. Words cannot adequately state my respect for Nelson Mandela.

The annual Independence Day celebration in the Nation's capital is attended by thousands who assemble on the Mall. In 1990, I sang at this celebration with Rostropovich and the National Symphony Orchestra. Beverly Sills served as mistress of ceremonies, and Tom Foley presented me with a beautiful vase for my participation. What a meaningful, moving evening!

Another highlight was performing with Audrey Hepburn and Gregory Peck in Oslo, Norway in 1990, when the Elie Wiesel Foundation for Humanity and the Nobel Peace Prize Committee sponsored a conference on "The Anatomy of Hate"—why it exists and how we can overcome it.

Participants included former President Jimmy Carter, President Vaclav Havel from the Czech Republic (then Czechoslovakia), Nelson Mandela, and French President François Mitterand. The King and Queen of Norway held a reception at the Palace for all who had attended the conference. To be asked to perform for such great people was for me an honor.

In 1993, I sang at the 300th anniversary of the opera house in Leipzig, Germany. As a man of color, I was deeply moved to be asked to sing the title role of the Russian opera *Boris Godunov* in Germany's oldest opera house. The evening was very well received by the people of Leipzig.

In October 1994, I sang for Nobel Laureate Archbishop Desmond Tutu at the Cathedral of St. John the Divine in New York. We talked about my upcoming appearance in South Africa and the impossibility of this even being a remote opportunity just a few years ago.

I felt proud to sing for the 25th anniversary of the United Nations in 1970. I was honored to be invited back for the 50th anniversary in October 1995. The audience included the late Yitzhak Rabin, Nelson Mandela, Yassar Arafat, and Boris Yeltsin.

November 1998 marked my 100th role and my Washington (D.C.) Opera debut in the title role of Verdi's *Simon Boccanegra*. I had previously sung the role of Fiesco in this opera. However, when Placido Domingo and I sang together in a *Carmen* production (he was Don José and I was Escamillo), Placido was really enthusiastic about my singing and engaged me for the title role of Simon Boccanegra in the opera house he directs.

Zurich. When I first traveled to Zurich in 1975, little did I realize my future was etched in the traditions and spirit of this remarkable city. I made this trip at the urging of Ferdinand Leitner for whom I sang at the Chicago Lyric Opera. "Go to Zurich and audition for the new intendant, Dr. Helmut Claus Drese. You will like him. He has new ideas and is looking for talent. You have an outstanding voice that would please European audiences."

I headed for Switzerland to meet this man who eventually became a good friend and colleague. After my audition, he asked me to return the following season to debut in *Macbeth*. This posed a problem because my friend Norman Mittelman was then singing that title role. Norman and I met when we both were performing for the Chicago Lyric Opera. We sang together in other cities and became friends. I could not displace a friend despite the importance of the job to my career.

"I would like to accept your offer," I explained to Dr. Drese, "but my very good friend Norman is singing it now and I would be uncomfortable taking his role. Perhaps I could do Banquo."

I preferred the smaller part of Banquo because Norman could continue as Macbeth and I could have a role as well.

Amazed, he said, "I have never met anyone who would give up an opportunity like this in the name of friendship. You are very unusual. Next spring we will be doing a new production of *Macbeth*. I want you in the title role for that season. For now, I have nothing to offer. Perhaps you would come back and see me." I thanked him for his time and understanding.

In 1976, we visited again when I returned to Zurich. Dr. Drese offered me the role of Porgy in *Porgy and Bess* for my Zurich debut.

"Thank you very much, but I must decline your offer," I told him, hoping to gain his understanding a second time. "Since I have never sung in this city, I feel it would be a mistake to begin with that role. I want to sing a variety of roles in the future, not just those for blacks only, and I feel this would stereotype me so I would not be believable in other parts."

Dr. Drese nodded sympathetically. "I understand. We will be doing Wagner's *The Flying Dutchman* in the fall. Would opening the season in that opera interest you?"

I assumed he had in mind the lesser role of Daland. I never dreamed he would say, "I want you for the Dutchman's role."

The lead! What an incredible turn of events! I certainly couldn't refuse this offer. I agreed to do Porgy in the spring and open the fall season with *The Flying Dutchman*.

It seemed the best decision at the time, but I later regretted doing Porgy first.

"I accept, but I want to sign the contracts for both now."

He smiled. "You are a clever man."

"Business is business," I said, "and I want to make sure both are signed now."

My performance as The Flying Dutchman made me the first black man to appear on stage at the prestigious Bayreuth Festival.

Bayreuth. Before the fall premiere, I went to Bayreuth, Germany, to audition with Wolfgang Wagner (the grandson of Richard Wagner) for the Dutchman role in a new production for the 1978 season. As the site of the annual Wagner festival, Bayreuth is known throughout the opera world as "the place" for Wagner aficionados.

Wagner liked my voice and offered me two roles: the Dutchman in *The Flying Dutchman* and Amfortas in *Parsifal*. I was the first black man to sing at this prestigious opera festival. One Hamburg journalist predicted in his column that I would be booed because I was black. That didn't happen; it was a wonderful experience.

This began a long association with Bayreuth which lasted until 1985. I enjoyed singing in Bayreuth because of the professional atmosphere and Wolfgang Wagner's excellence in organizing the entire production.

In 1983, Bayreuth scheduled Wagner's *Ring Cycle* (which consists of the four operas *Das Rheingold*, *Die Walküre*, *Siegfried*, and *Die Götterdämmerung*) under the direction of a prominent conductor and stage director. I drove to Munich with my accompanist to audition for the role of Wotan in *Die Walküre*. The conductor and his secretary settled in to hear me sing King Philip's lament from the opera *Don Carlo* and Wotan's "Abschied" or "Farewell." When I finished, the conductor stated, "I don't need to hear anything else. That was fantastic. You have a magnificent voice and your musicianship is superb."

He paused, looked at me and hurled the thunderbolt. "How do you expect to sing Wotan in Bayreuth—being a black?"

I was speechless. I could not believe a man of his stature in the musical world would say this. He wanted to avoid the controversy he thought my presence would generate.

I finally responded, "I've been singing the Dutchman in Bayreuth for the last five years with no problems."

"That doesn't count because it is a myth," the conductor shot back.

I chose not to discuss this, because the entire *Ring Cycle* is a myth. "The public has not reacted in a negative manner when I've sung before. I did Amfortas in *Parsifal* and the audience reaction was extremely favorable."

"I don't want any problems and the stage director does not want a black Wotan."

To myself, I thought, "Why did you have me make this trip if you had already decided I could not have the role?"

He told me the role suited me vocally and musically. He even said my voice was magnificent. Still in shock, I said, "Wolfgang Wagner is not against my singing Wotan."

"I'm not sure about that," he replied.

"He's been happy with my work. Traditionally, men who sing the Dutchman can sing Wotan."

The conductor offered to give my audition some thought, but he was not optimistic. He did say he would talk to Wolfgang Wagner.

His remarks bothered me for months. When we both happened to be vacationing in Italy, I found an opportunity to visit. "I would like to speak to you man to man. Not black to white, not conductor to singer, just man to man," I began. "I would like to talk without any interruptions." He nodded.

"For some time, your reaction to my skin color when I auditioned for you has surprised and dismayed me. Composers wrote for voices, not skin color. In the front of no score does it say singers must be white, yellow, or black. Composers wrote for a certain voice: soprano, mezzo, baritone, tenor. In our art, color shouldn't matter, except for coloring and shading one's voice. You asked me why I wanted to sing Wagner's music with my beautiful voice. Why do you want to conduct music that is so beautiful? When a composer wrote with such beauty for strings and other instruments, he wanted beautiful voices. Furthermore, no one comments when Placido Domingo sings Othello or when Caballé or Tebaldi or some other lady not of color sings Aida."

"Excuse me," he said. "I can honestly say I never really thought of that."

"Patrons don't look at color. They are not upset if a person of color sings a role. In *Madame Butterfly*, nobody objects if an Italian or American instead of an Asian sings the leading role." I paused. "Thank you for listening to how I feel."

After a moment, he said, "I thought if I could eliminate a controversy, why shouldn't I do it?"

"But I am the one who has suffered because of this."

"You've convinced me that color shouldn't matter. I must audition one other person, but you have the inside curve. However, the stage director does not want a black Wotan. He says if we have a black Wotan, everyone has to be black and he can't find enough black singers. Would you come and audition for the two of us?"

I swallowed my pride and said, "Yes."

True to his word, he called. I was busy, but this was so important that I flew to London to audition for both men. The entire time I sang, the stage director never looked at me or made any eye contact. When I finished, he made one statement: "Well, your voice is certainly too big for this room. Will someone call a taxi?"

With that he abruptly stood and left. The conductor thanked me for coming and said he would be in touch with me.

The next day, my agent at Columbia Artists Management received a message from the conductor reading, "Simon, I'm sorry I will not be able to accept you as Wotan. It has nothing to do with your musicianship or your voice. Please accept my admiration for your talent, and at my earliest possible convenience, I will engage you with my orchestra."

When I returned to Bayreuth the next summer, Wolfgang Wagner was incredulous as I described the events. "I can't believe this! Simon, I would never have engaged you in the past if color was an issue."

In my mind there was no doubt that color was the factor. What else could it have been when the conductor's telegram stated that my not getting the role had nothing to do with my voice or musicianship?

Upset himself, Wagner asked me not to go to the press. I didn't. They came to me. I told Wagner I would not lie because people need to

know the degree of discrimination against people of color in opera. If I talked to the press, others would become aware of this problem.

I regret to say that their production of *Die Walküre* failed. The audience booed the conductor and stage manager, and the conductor did not return to Bayreuth the next year.

Ironically, some years previous, a young man fled his native country and journeyed to Zurich, Switzerland. He had no money, but he had talent. He had no studio, but my former wife's grandparents invited him to use their piano for lessons so he could support himself. His career flourished and he became one of the best known conductors in the music world. This was the same conductor who was reluctant to hire me.

Bayreuth served as one of the great catalysts in my career. After my initial performance, many European houses invited me to perform.

I would have returned to Bayreuth every year,

Appearing at the Orange Festival as Orestes in "Elektra" gave me the opportunity to expand my repertoire.

but I wanted to sing in other festivals, such as the one in Orange.

Orange. Every summer Les Chorégies d'Orange (France) presents several operas in the historic Théatre Antique which was built in the days of Augustus and seats 8,000 people. Carefully restored, it is well known for its exceptional acoustics. I hope the entertainment in ancient times outweighed the agony of sitting on those concrete tiers. Every seat is occupied during a performance, suggesting the audience must not mind the lack of comfort.

Orange is such a pleasant place in the summer. Citizens go out of their way to make the opera cast feel welcome, and the countryside looks like a Van Gogh painting complete with rich fields of sunflowers and lavender. My colleagues and I always look forward to singing there.

Leading ladies. One of the greatest moments in my career occurred in 1984 when I sang with Leontyne Price. For her farewell performance at the Metropolitan Opera House in New York, she sang the title role in Verdi's *Aida* and I sang the role of her father Amonasro. I was proud to be part of this memorable occasion.

We previously had sung these roles together in San Francisco. At one of our rehearsals, she began crying. "Excuse me Simon, but it's such an honor to sing with you," she explained.

Leontyne's words moved me. "No, no, it's just the opposite," I exclaimed. "It is *my* honor to sing with you."

She regained her composure and the rehearsal continued. Later she explained, "Besides the quality of your voice, it is an additional honor to be singing with a black man."

Although Marian Anderson sang at the Met, it was Leontyne who broke the color barrier for all singers, male and female. Both women endured so very, very much.

Leontyne once shared with me how she had suffered because of threats on her life when she opened at the Met. "Simon, it's going to be even more difficult for you. Because you are a black male, the discrimination will be greater. You have a beautiful voice, you are musical, intelligent, independent, and handsome. With all those ingredients, you are a threat. It will be more difficult for you than it was for me."

Both Leontyne and I have commented on discrimination, especially in our field. Her prophetic message is true: "When one tells the truth, it really hurts." My comments on black singers and their lack of roles have caused some orchestras and operas to shun me. For several years, I didn't sing as often in the United States.

Singing with Simon Estes in *Aida* made me feel just wonderful, having this "black god" standing behind me.

— Leontyne Price

With Leontyne Price in her farewell performance at the Metropolitan Opera House in New York City

Another moving experience came when I sang at the Metropolitan Opera House with Birgit Nilsson, regarded by many as the greatest Wagnerian soprano of our time. After we finished the last big scene of *Die Walküre*, she offered one of the finest compliments given me during my singing career. "You are the greatest Wotan with whom I've ever sung. Your voice is more beautiful than that of any other Wotans with whom I have sung." The compliments from Birgit Nilsson and Leontyne Price were as wonderful as working with them. I also enjoyed singing with Joan Sutherland who had an incredible vocal technique and was an excellent artist. She was a great colleague.

All three of these ladies were not complicated. They did not behave as prima donnas. They were considered the greatest voices in their particular category, yet they were secure within themselves, down-to-earth, and a joy to know.

Role models. Professionally, I have been influenced by two role models: Leontyne Price and Paul Robeson, an African-American and the son of a slave. He was a bass-baritone classical singer and a recognized scholar, lawyer, athlete, and actor. Paul saw his gifts and success as a means to helping others. As a political activist, he proclaimed peace and social justice. He supported the independence of African colonies, but eventually paid a high price both personally and professionally for his involvement in these issues.

It seems fitting that Paul Robeson's epitaph came from a 1937 London speech in which he took a stand against fascism: "The artist must elect to fight for freedom or slavery. I have made my choice. I had no alternative."

The Repertoire

The opera roles I most enjoy singing are the most dramatic in terms of vocal stamina, power, ability, and range. Their demanding nature plays into why I am engaged to sing these roles and why I love the challenges they present. Wotan, the Dutchman, and Porgy are all long roles. With the exception of Porgy, my skin color might not make me first choice in many operas; however, the major factor is my ability to sing the roles.

Although I tend to focus on traditional opera, I've also performed Schubert, Mahler, Brahms songs, Mozart concert arias, and I've sung close to 50 orchestral works. I love to sing orchestral and sacred works like Bach's *St. Matthew's Passion* or Beethoven's *Ninth Symphony*. Singing *The Missa Solemnis*, a Beethoven mass, is a religious experience. I've sung and recorded requiems in several languages: Brahms in German, Verdi and Fauré in Latin, Britten and DeMars in English. My repertoire also includes Haydn's *Creation* and Handel's *Messiah*.

Among the 100 different opera roles I have sung, several stand out as favorites, because I identify with the character and love the music vocally. Not all are admirable characters, but most have redeeming qualities. I immerse myself in a role to the extent that I "become" that character during the performance.

When I change my physical appearance from Simon Estes to Wotan or Macbeth, for example, I'm still aware of who I am and where I've come from. Sometimes I think back on that skinny little kid from Centerville, Iowa who never dreamed he would get farther east than Chicago.

After the performance when I walk into my dressing room and remove my makeup and

I've had the honor of singing Porgy on stages throughout the world with leading ladies such as Laverne Williams and Grace Bumbry. Perhaps none was more satisfying than the long-awaited premiere at New York City's Metropolitan Opera House.

George Gershwin Gets His Due

After 50 years *Porgy and Bess* arrives at the Metropolitan Opera

George Gershwin maintained that *Porgy and Bess* was a real opera, not a glorified Broadway musical, but until recently, few believed him. Early productions generally truncated his ample (more than three hours) score, cut down its lush orchestration and substituted spoken dialogue for the recitatives. But there has been growing interest in an authentic *Porgy*, beginning with the Houston Grand Opera's 1976 production and followed by an even more opulent version seen at New York's Radio City Music Hall two years ago. Last week, 50 years after its premiere, *Porgy* came all the way uptown to the Metropolitan Opera. At last, the work's operatic pretensions have been fairly and thoroughly tested. And you know what? Gershwin was almost right.

Already *Porgy* is the hottest ticket in town; all 16 scheduled performances were sold out even before the opening. The piece's unique claim to be the American national opera is partly responsible, of course, as is the curiosity value associated with any first. But the Met delivers the goods. In the hands of a major conductor, *Porgy and Bess* the

Estes and Bumbry as Porgy and Bess
Fights, crowds and a slice-of-life vigor.

Doctor Jesus, in which six independent musical lines, notated without bars, move against a hummed background,

The soloist Soprano Grac fails to comm try eroticism ture. Better dignified, s voice is not jured durin the cripple vidual ho ence Quiv dashing Crown. rected b Merrill as Dou umph. Dance with t stage of-lif

lack Por her stra co re ca t s

I like to sing Amonasro in "Aida" because, even though it is a short role on stage, it is a major role vocally.

PRESENTS

RICHARD

STRAUSS'

SALOME

CONDUCTED BY RICHARD BRADSHAW   DIRECTED BY ATOM EGOYAN

ER 27 > OCTOBER 19, 1996

CENTRE, TORONTO

.2262

$30 > $100

SALOMÉ SPONSORED BY

As Sarastro in "The Magic Flute," I enjoy a great variety of music, from noble and uplifting to sentimental.

costume, the role comes off, too. I am Simon Estes, not Wotan or King Philip or the Flying Dutchman.

Favorite roles. The role that catapulted my career and with which I have been identified most frequently is Wagner's Flying Dutchman. I've sung this role about 400 times. The fascinating Dutchman sails around the world for eternity, allowed to come ashore once every seven years to find the woman who can redeem him through love and be true to him forever.

Gershwin's *Porgy and Bess* is very well known throughout the world. The characters represent the reality of their society, which Gershwin experienced when he spent time in South Carolina learning the speech patterns and the music of the black residents. This opera differs from many other popular operas because it is based on real life, not myth.

It tells the story of Porgy, a poor cripple, and his love for Bess. *Porgy and Bess* deals with despair and grief, but also with hope. I rank this opera with *The Flying Dutchman* and *Die Walküre*.

I was deeply honored to have sung Porgy in New York City at the Metropolitan Opera's first performance ever in 1985 (it premiered there 50 years after its opening at New York's Alvin Theatre).

I also performed this role in Zurich, Switzerland, Tulsa, Oklahoma in the United

Musically and vocally, King Philip in "Don Carlo" is an extremely rewarding role, which some regard as the best bass-baritone role Verdi ever wrote.

Each of the characters I portray in "The Tales of Hoffmann" has a common trait which is the antithesis of my own character—a devil's soul that conquers through fear rather than love.

I first sang Boris Godunov in late 1973 and had 53 curtain calls!

States, and in 1996, in Cape Town, South Africa, with many local black artists who sang in the opera house for the first time.

Wotan in Richard Wagner's *Die Walküre* also ranks high on my list of favorite roles. The beginning of the opera finds Wotan very proud of his daughter Brünnhilde. As the opera progresses, he becomes not only a broken man, but also the talkative confessing father to Brünnhilde. Although she knows her actions will incur his wrath, she disobeys the implicit instructions he has given her. An angry Wotan condemns Brünnhilde. At the end of the opera, Wotan is filled with sorrow. The role runs the full gamut of emotions, all vocally challenging.

Another father role I enjoy is Amonasro in Verdi's opera *Aida*. Captured by the Egyptians, this deposed King of Ethiopia is reunited with his enslaved daughter Aida. He persuades her to entice her lover Radames, an Egyptian captain, to betray his country and help free the Ethiopians. I like to sing Amonasro because, even though it's a short role, it's a major role vocally. The part of Amonasro contains music that is most gratifying.

Verdi's opera *Nabucco* ranks as another favorite. In *Nabucco,* I usually play Zaccaria, the Hebrew High Priest who helps his people after they have been captured by Nabucco's armies. In 1995, I performed the title role in Cape Town, South Africa.

A character with whom I easily identify is Amfortas in Wagner's *Parsifal*. This very religious work combines pagan mythology and Christianity. Amfortas, the badly wounded ruler of the Knights of the Grail, can only be healed by one man and one remedy: Parsifal and the Holy Spear. The opera presents the concept of spiritual redemption through a savior victorious over evil. The ending is incredibly uplifting.

John the Baptist (Jochanaan) in Strauss' *Salome* is another role with spiritual significance for me because he is a messenger of God. I feel very religious when I play John, even though Strauss took a very liberal view of the Bible. The beautiful Salome catches the eye of Herod, who has been warned of terrible consequences if he looks upon her too ardently. Ignoring this warning, Herod offers Salome one wish.

She has John beheaded, and the opera ends with my head on a platter.

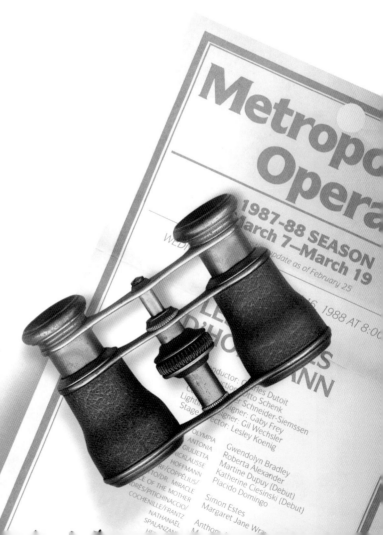

The Flying Dutchman role catapulted my career; I have sung it almost 400 times.

I enjoy singing the part of Escamillo in Georges Bizet's "Carmen," especially the well-known "Toreador song."

When I change my appearance from Simon Estes to a character such as Landgraf in "Tannhäuser" I'm still very much aware of who I am.

I enjoy singing the part of Escamillo in Georges Bizet's *Carmen*, especially the well-known "Toreador Song." In this popular opera, the beautiful gypsy Carmen seduces Corporal Don Jose away from his regiment only to leave him for Escamillo, a toreador who has been pursuing her. This opera is a joy to sing because of the vivid music, continuously flowing melody, and brilliant orchestration.

I enjoy the role of Baron Scarpia, the ruthless chief of police in Puccini's *Tosca*. Scarpia is a dark soul willing to torture a painter, Cavaradossi, so he can have his way with Tosca, Cavaradossi's lover. At the same time, Scarpia is fulfilling his duties as chief of police—Cavaradossi stands accused of helping a political prisoner escape. Part of the challenge of this role lies in presenting Scarpia as an evil villain.

Another favorite, Mozart's *The Magic Flute*, is a charming fairy tale containing a great variety of music, from noble and uplifting to sentimental. I sing the role of Sarastro who kidnaps Pamina to protect her from her evil mother the queen. The queen in return sends a knight to rescue her daughter. However, the knight is in love with Pamina and Sarastro arranges their marriage, thwarting the queen's evil plans.

King Philip, the father in Verdi's opera *Don Carlo,* is another interesting favorite. In a disagreement, Don Carlo draws his sword to challenge his father, King Philip. The Grand Inquisitor demands Don Carlo's death for that action, which he sees as treason. Philip feels loyalty to his son, but he also feels that as King he cannot be above the law. The duet between Philip and the Grand Inquisitor expresses the differences in the characters—one weak, one strong. Another conflict centers on Don Carlo's love for the fair Elisabetta, whom his father took for a bride.

Musically and vocally, King Philip is an extremely rewarding role which some regard as the best bass-baritone role Verdi ever wrote. I agree with that assessment, and I consider *Don Carlo* to be Verdi's best opera. It requires excellent voices for each of the six roles—Don Carlo, King Philip, Elisabetta, Rodrigo, the Grand Inquisitor, and Princess Eboli—with each character performing a beautiful and demanding aria or duet. In addition, this opera is considerably more symphonic than some of Verdi's other works.

The Tales of Hoffmann presents an interesting challenge—I play four characters (Lindorf, Coppelius, Dapertutto, and Dr. Miracle) during this opera about a poet's attempts to find love. The evil Lindorf and his three alternate personalities steal away each of Hoffmann's four loves and leave him a broken drunken man. Each of the characters I portray has a common trait which is the antithesis of my own character—a devil's soul that conquers through fear rather than love.

I love playing Macbeth from Verdi's opera adaptation of Shakespeare's play. I find this long and exciting baritone role challenging. Macbeth is a very sick and demented soul and, in opera circles, it is rumored that people who are a little evil themselves have a difficult time singing Macbeth. However I can easily remember this is only an opera!

Moussorgsky's *Boris Godunov* is one of the most famous Russian operas. Although as hungry for power as Macbeth, Boris possesses some redeeming qualities as a father.

I first sang Boris in Lübeck, Germany in 1973 and we had 53 curtain calls! In 1993, I sang it again at the Leipzig Opera House for the 300 years celebration of the opening of this famous opera house.

Themes and Variations

During my American engagements, I see a great deal of the country and meet people from all backgrounds. These small towns form the backbone of our country. When European friends travel to the United States, I urge them to experience these communities to get a sense of the richness and genuineness of America.

Some of my own great memories center around unscheduled events that took place when I gave concerts in those small towns.

After my accompanist and I arrived in a small Arizona town, we checked the concert hall and discovered the piano keys stuck when played. "Is another piano available?" I asked politely.

"Sorry, no," replied the hall manager, looking visibly embarrassed.

We had to find a replacement for this clearly unusable piano. "Would you please call high schools in neighboring towns and ask if we could borrow a piano for tonight?"

He located a piano and we borrowed a truck and blanket and took off. As students helped us load the piano, we realized that in our haste, we forgot to bring any rope. On our return trip, I stood in the back with the piano and struggled to keep it and me from falling out of the truck. We returned without any serious incidents, and after a quick tune-up, we were ready for the concert. It was the only time in my career when I helped transport my own piano.

In another town, a thick layer of dust covered the piano, so I asked, "Would you please dust the piano before our concert this evening?"

That night my accompanist sat down to play and his hands flew across the keys in a glissando which startled him—and me. Anxious to please us, someone had oiled every key.

A terrible snowstorm delayed my arrival to one concert, leaving the audience waiting patiently. Just before I made my entrance, I sneezed wrong, which caused me to cough for about 15 minutes and delay the concert even more. With two strikes against me, I went for three. I started singing "I've Got Plenty of Nothin'"—and that is exactly what I had: "Nothin.'" I had forgotten the lyrics.

I stopped, looked at the audience, and admitted, "Guess what? I've forgotten the words, so I'm going to stand behind my accompanist and read over his shoulders." The audience loved it!

Male singers' greatest fear is not that our voices will fail us, but that our zippers will. One evening as I walked out with my accompanist and took a bow, I discovered that not only were my pants unzipped, but also part of my shirttail stuck out.

Embarrassed, I turned sideways to walk off the stage. As I passed my accompanist, I whispered, "My pants are unzipped."

In hindsight, I should have just turned my back to the audience to zip my pants. Instead, I went out the stage door, zipped my pants, and turned to reenter. Lo and behold, the door had locked behind me!

My concert repertoire includes classical, religious, spirituals, show tunes, and contemporary music. Three pieces hold very special meaning for me. "Climb Ev'ry Mountain," from the musical "The Sound of Music," is about people having a dream and forging ahead regardless of difficulties. "Ol' Man River," from "Showboat," says we all struggle along a great river, and we must continue to struggle in life to reach a great goal. "God Bless America" reminds us that America is about all of us living together, loving each other, and remembering that love comes from God.

2
CLIMB EV'RY MOUNTAIN
(From "THE SOUND OF MUSIC")
Lyrics by OSCAR HAMMERSTEIN II
Music by RICHARD RODGERS
Maestoso
ff
rit.
C
D7
Climb
ev
mf a tempo
Fmaj7
low,
Dm7
ev
2
Ol' Man River
Words by
OSCAR HAMMERSTEIN II
Music by
JEROME KERN
Moderato
Piano
ff deliberato
2
GOD BLESS AMERICA
(LOW VOICE)
Low in D (A to B)
Words and Music by
IRVING BERLIN
Moderato
f
Let us swear al-
Far a-cross the sea,
VOICE
ad lib.
While the storm clouds gath-er
ad lib.
mf
For a land so
Let us all be grate-ful
To a land that's free,
le-giance
In a sol-emn prayer.
As we raise our voi-ces
a tempo

No one, not even a stagehand, was backstage. I knocked on the door but no one heard me. Feeling frantic, I knocked even harder, with no response. The audience waited and so did my accompanist. I had no choice but to find the front door.

I went outside, walked around the building, and found the main entrance. I surprised the audience and shocked my accompanist when I entered from the back of the concert hall and walked past the concertgoers. When I told the audience the whole story, they laughed, and laughed some more. It was quite an icebreaker. The concert turned out to be one of my best.

I have stayed in scores of small hotels and motels throughout America and several stand out in my memory. Many serve the best bacon-and-eggs breakfast in the world, such as the one my accompanist and I enjoyed in Nebraska. When the waitress saw that his cup needed to be refilled, she asked, "Can I touch up your coffee?"

And "touch it up" she did. Instead of picking up the cup by the handle, she stuck her thumb inside the cup to lift and refill it.

Owners of a motel in the Southwestern part of the United States proudly offered me their only suite complete with blue concrete floors, a broken-down sofa in one room, and a bed in the other. I thanked them profusely for giving me their best rooms, and I appreciated their gracious effort to be accommodating.

I love staying in those little motels, but I wonder why they all have bathroom exhaust fans that could pull you right off your feet.

Frequently after I have sung Brahms, Wolf, or Mahler in a recital, audiences request an encore. At the conclusion of one concert, a man approached me, shook my hand, and said, "You know, after having heard you sing today, guess what song I think you really should sing."

Curious, I replied, "I don't know."

"Oh, come on. You know."

"I'm sorry. I really don't know."

"With your voice, you could sing a song like 'Shortnin' Bread.' It was written just for you."

Racial discrimination is a fact of life for me, professionally as well as personally, in small towns, large cities, and occasionally other countries. My career has led me to wonderful people and rewarding experiences which far outweigh the negative. But discrimination remains a challenge I must contend with and cannot allow to hold me back.

Simon Estes is one of the greatest artists in the world. For the past 20 years, it has been my privilege to have the stage with him.

— Julius Tilghman
Accompanist

ÄNGER IM HISTORISCHEN GEBÄUDE DER PO

IMON
STES

ss - Bariton

Broadway
Hits
& Spirituals

Tilghman am Flügel

Mai 1998 - 20.00 Uhr

m Stephansplatz Eingang Dammtorwall 4

egenüber der Staatsoper)

METROPOLITAN OPERA · NEW YORK
SAN FRANCISCO OPERA
CHICAGO LYRIC OPERA
BAYREUTH WAGNER FESTIVALS
VIENNA STAATSOPER
LA SCALA · MILAN
PARIS OPERA
DEUTSCHE OPER · BERLIN
BAYERISCHE STAATSOPER · MUNICH
HAMBURG STAATSOPER
STÄDTISCHE BÜHNEN · FRANKFURT
MAGGIO MUSICALE FIORENTINO

SIMON ESTES
BASS-BARITONE

Julius has traveled with me throughout Europe and the United States. His humor always entertains me, and his rich philosophical discussions keep my mind in tune.

Simon Estes

Since winning the First International Tchaikovsky Competition in Moscow, Iowa-born bass-baritone SIMON ESTES has become one of the world's most acclaimed operatic stars. His appearances at Bayreuth, the Metropolitan, La Scala, the Vienna State Opera, San Francisco, and every other leading opera house in the world have set a standard that is his alone. Long noted as a most compelling recitalist, the handsome 6'1" singing-actor has also lent his name and given his talent towards numerous humanitarian causes.

COLUMBIA ARTISTS MANAGEMENT INC.

Personal Direction: DAVID V. FOSTER / Associate: Hattie Clark   165 West 57th Street, New York, NY 10019

83GF   491 PRINTED IN U.S.A.

In the 1960s and '70s, blacks were asked to sing in the South if they sang jazz, gospel, or rock; if a black sang opera, that was a different story. Michael Ries, my CAMI manager, warned me, "The South is not ready for black opera singers." He was right. Those were difficult years. I once gave a concert to 25 people in a hall that held 1000.

In the early 1970s, my accompanist and I rented a car to drive to a performance. A highway patrolman followed us from the airport into town. At lunch time, that same patrolman approached our table and asked, What are you doing here?"

"I'm performing a concert. I'm an opera singer and this is my accompanist."

"Uh, huh. You drove down here, didn't ya?"

"Yes, we did. You should know that because you followed us. Why did you do that?"

"Jus' doin' my job. I'll be watching you." With that warning, he walked away.

Not surprisingly, that was the town where only 25 people came to my concert.

The manager of a major Southern opera told me, "I think your voice is beautiful and I would love to engage you, but I would lose the support of my governing board and many patrons if I hired a black to sing in an opera."

"I really respect your truthfulness," I replied. "From a business point of view I understand, but from a moral point of view I disagree heartily. Blacks should be allowed to sing more than jazz or gospel down here, and people have the right to hear blacks sing opera. Then they could tell their children that here is a black man who is not an athlete but an opera singer." He agreed, but he still couldn't book me.

During one concert in the South, I was the only black guest at a particular hotel. Dressed in tails for my concert, I stepped onto the elevator. A white lady in the elevator glared at me.

"Hey, boy, what did you do with them?" she demanded.

I wanted to ignore her, but her attitude demanded some kind of response.

"I have no idea what you are talking about, ma'am," I replied.

"We know you took them."

"Excuse me, but I don't understand to what you are referring," I said politely. The word "took" flashed a warning.

"You stole a lady's jewelry."

"I'm on my way to sing in a concert."

"That don't make no difference to me. We're going to search everything and every place in your room."

I replied, "Let me tell you something, ma'am. You may search my room, but when I come back, everything had better be in order. I didn't steal the lady's jewelry, whoever she is and whatever jewelry she had.

"Besides, if I wanted jewelry, I could afford to buy my own."

With that parting remark, I left the elevator. When I returned after the concert, it was obvious that my room had been searched. I did not inquire if the thief had been apprehended, and I was not offered any apology nor explanation for the room search.

To this woman, my skin color signaled "thief."

In another city, the waitress glared at me as I entered the hotel coffee shop with Harold Brown, my accompanist, a white man. She obviously did not want to wait on me. She turned to Harold, took his order, then asked me, "What ya want?"

When the black male cook called that our orders were ready, the waitress served Harold but left my pancakes on the order counter. After the cook's third call, she sauntered over to the counter, brought the plate to me, slammed it on the table, and turned to leave.

I checked the cakes. "Excuse me, ma'am. These cakes are cold."

She was furious. She grabbed the plate. "They can't be; the plate's warm."

"The plate may be warm," I said evenly, "but the pancakes are cold. My order was ready at the same time as my companion's. You left it sitting because you didn't want to serve me. I'm going to ask you kindly to bring me hot pancakes."

The cook, watching and listening to the exchange, gave a small smile and turned to start another order. The waitress snatched away my plate with such anger that I thought those pancakes would sail across the room, but they were too cold to move. She turned in another order and this time brought them reasonably warm. Harold and I were more than ready to check out of this particular hotel.

When I stayed in motels in the South during the 1960s and '70s, I always propped a chair under the door handle, thinking that if someone tried to force the door, I might have a chance to escape through a window. I didn't want to be a martyr, but I felt obliged to sing in the South. People there needed the opportunity to know a black man can sing opera as well as jazz. But with each appearance, I couldn't wait for the airplane to take off and deliver me.

In the early 1970s, I appeared with an American opera company for ten weeks. I bought a Mercedes-Benz at the factory in Germany and had it shipped to the States. A brand new Mercedes with a black man at the wheel was a red flag to the local police, and in those ten weeks they stopped me ten times.

The first time, I was on my way to a rehearsal. After I pulled over, the policeman knocked vigorously on my car window. I lowered it.

"Give me your driver's license," he growled.

"What is the problem, officer?"

"You don't have any license plates for this car."

"Oh, no! Somebody must have stolen them," I said and opened the door to investigate. The international plates were to remain on the car while I awaited delivery of my Iowa plates.

"Don't open that door!" he barked. "Stay in the car."

"I just wanted to look because the plates were there this morning," I tried to explain.

"There are plates, but they aren't valid."

"I don't understand," I protested. "The manufacturer assured me I could use the international plates until my new ones arrive."

The policeman ignored my explanation and continued his line of questioning. "Do you have papers for this car?"

I handed him the registration.

"I mean the bill of sale. I want proof that this is your car." His voice revealed his irritation.

"I don't have the bill of sale for this car. Who carries that around?" Then it dawned on me. "Oh! You think I stole this car. Are you upset because I am driving this Mercedes and I am a black man? I did not steal this car. I paid for it."

He became extremely angry. "Stay in your car. I'm taking you to the station." He called for a backup and, with one car in front of me and one in back, we drove to the nearest station.

Simon Estes
Bass-Baritone

Front Photo: James Heffernan
Back Photo: Philips Classics Productions   Philips Records

COLUMBIA ARTISTS MANAGEMENT INC.
Personal Direction: RONALD A. WILFORD and LAURENCE E. TUCKER
165 West 57th Street, New York, NY 10019

FDF86

Printed in US

The officer informed his captain that I was driving without license plates.

Again, I explained. I added that I was singing with the opera company, but he either didn't believe me or didn't care. "You're going to jail unless you post bail," the captain told me.

Luckily, they allowed me one phone call. I reached the opera house manager, who advised me to contact the opera house lawyer. "This is obviously harassment," the lawyer told me. "Do you have $25 with you? Give it to them so you don't have to go to jail. We'll take care of the rest." I paid the money and left.

During the next nine weeks, police officers stopped me nine more times. They charged that I had run a red light, though my passenger insisted I had not. They accused me of speeding although I hadn't been. The last five or six times they pulled me over, I told each officer, "I have been stopped by your colleagues several times and I have broken no laws. You know I haven't this time, so why are you stopping me?"

I never received a ticket, but it was very difficult and uncomfortable knowing they might stop me at any time.

The threat. During a most enjoyable overseas tour, I wanted to write my mother and friends at home about the friendly people and successful concerts. I left my hotel, crossed the street, and headed toward a card and souvenir shop to purchase postcards.

Two men in suits suddenly came up right behind me. One stepped to my right and one to my left. "May we see some identification?" they asked.

Startled by their sudden appearance, I inquired, "For what reason? Who are you?"

"We're asking the questions." These men wore office attire, not uniforms. Dressed in a Pierre Cardin jacket and slacks, I clearly wasn't a bum.

Once again I asked, "Who are you?" Each man whipped out his police identification.

"Is there a problem?"

"You look like an escaped convict."

"I'm an American citizen," I countered.

"Let's see your passport."

With a sick sinking feeling, I realized I had left it behind. "I do have a driver's license plus some credit cards which should identify me. I left my passport in my hotel right across the street."

One of the men impatiently ordered, "You don't tell us things. We do all the talking. Where are you from?"

"I am an American here with [a national commission]. My hotel is just across the street."

"You are coming with us." I assumed this meant they would accompany me to my hotel for my proof of citizenship. They asked me to get into a car. I did so and they started driving toward my hotel.

As we drove past it, I said, "Wait! There's my hotel!"

"Shut up."

"I thought you were taking me there so I could get my passport." Then I became upset and angry and frightened. I began to wonder if their credentials were real. "Where are we going?"

"Downtown to headquarters."

"For what?"

"We told you. You look like an escaped convict."

"Would an escaped convict be walking around in Pierre Cardin clothes?"

Again, they told me to shut up and not get smart with them. When we arrived at their headquarters, I was very apprehensive. It looked far too important to be a normal jail house.

Inside, they took me into a room and began to interrogate me. I asked if I could make a phone call, which is the procedure in America. "No."

SIMON ESTES ON THE INTERNATIONAL OPERA STAGE

1977
LA SCALA
BOLOGNA
SEATTLE
ZURICH

"Pelleas and Melisande"
"Oberto" (Verdi)
"Götterdämmerung"
"The Flying Dutchman"
"Porgy and Bess"
"Il Ritorno d'Ulisse" (Monteverdi)

1978
MUNICH

MODENA
PARMA
HAMBURG
ZURICH

BAYREUTH
VIENNA

ROUEN

"The Flying Dutchman"
"Elektra"
"Oberto"
"Oberto"
"Don Carlos"
"The Flying Dutchman"
"Il Ritorno d'Ulisse"
"The Flying Dutchman"
"The Flying Dutchman"
"The Magic Flute"
"Don Carlos"
"Faust"

1979
HAMBURG
ZURICH

LA SCALA
BAYREUTH
SAN FRANCISCO

"The Flying Dutchman"
"Il Ritorno d'Ulisse"
"Don Carlos"
"The Flying Dutchman"
"The Magic Flute"
"Mosé in Egitto" (Rossini)
"The Flying Dutchman"
"The Flying Dutchman"

1980
HAMBURG
ULSA
OSTON
URICH

"Macbeth"
"Die Walküre"
"The Flying Dutchman"
"Norma"
"Il Ritorno d'Ulisse"
"Attila"

981
RIS

"The Flying Dutchman"

Angel Records.
COLUMBIA ARTISTS
n: MICHAEL RIES/Asso
est 57th Street, New York

SLAURIE SEC E 1 7 COMP
EVENT CODE SECTION/AISLE ROW/BOX DUOR 3
ENTER SEAT
Price Incl. Sales Tax Adm. Incl. Sales Tax
$ .00 $ .00

SAN ANTONIO SYMPHONY
SEC E SIMON ESTES,
CA 6 X BASS-BARITONE
JAMES SEDARES, CONDUCTOR
1 7 LAURIE AUDITORIUM
ROW/BOX SEAT
SAS105 SAT. NOV 23,1985, 8:00PM
C17SEP5

Chicago Symphony Orchestra

Sir Georg Solti, *Music Director*

98th Season/Second Subscription Week

Thursday Evening, October 6, 1988, at 8:00
Friday Evening, October 7, 1988, at 8:00
Sunday Afternoon, October 9, 1988, at 3:00

The appearance of the soloists for this program has be n made possible in part through the generous support of the Brena and Lee A. Fr man, Sr., Vocal Soloist Fund.

SIR GEORG SOLTI   *Conductor*
SUSAN DUNN   *Soprano*
ROCHELLE ELLIS   *Soprano*
GIACOMO ARAGALL   *Tenor*
RICHARD COHN   *Baritone*
NICKOLAS KAROUSATOS   *Baritone*
LEO NUCCI   *Baritone*
SIMON ESTES   *Bass-Baritone*
CHICAGO SYMPHONY CHORUS
MARGARET HILLIS   *Director*

VERDI   *Simon Boccanegra,* Prol gue and Act I
(First Chicago Symphony O hestra performances)

Prologue: A Square in Ge oa

Intermission

Act I
   Scene I: The Garden of th
    Grimaldi, outside Genoa
   Scene II: The Council Cha ber in
    the Doge's Palace

OPERA DE PARIS BASTILLE
Porte 02 ESTES
Allee D
VAISSEAU FANTOME
1062288
11/10/93
LUNDI 19H30
570 F
RANG 20
PLACE 10
PARTERRE

Finally, I said to them, "I'm not going to answer any more questions until you call [the sponsoring organization] and confirm who I am." Once again they denied my request.

Both men were very rude and, for some reason, quite angry with me. Panic crept over me. Suddenly, without any explanation, the two men stood up and left the room.

On a table next to my chair, the front page of a newspaper carried my picture and an article about my concert with the city orchestra that evening. I flew to the door, newspaper in hand, to show them just who I was. As I put my foot outside the door, a man yelled, "Get back in that room."

"Wait, can I show you… "

"Get back in there!" I obeyed without arguing. I quickly reentered the room and sat down with the newspaper balanced on my lap, my own face staring back at me.

Another man came in and introduced himself as a captain. "Just calm down, young man. You're very argumentative today."

Slipping into the submissive black role and pointing to the paper, I said politely, "Look, here is my picture. I keep telling your men who I am, but they won't listen. If they would have let me stop at my hotel to get my passport, this misunderstanding would not have occurred. I thought that was what they were doing when they asked me to get into their car. I would really like to leave here. I have a performance tonight and right now I don't know if I will be able to sing because I am so upset." I knew I was babbling, but I couldn't stop because I was so afraid.

"You can leave," he said calmly and quietly.

"Thank you," I said in relief. "Could you please call the sponsoring commission to provide me with transportation back to my hotel? They've agreed to drive me during my stay here."

"My men will drive you back."

"No thank you." The last thing I wanted was to be in a car again with those two characters.

As we left the room, the captain searched for a taxi number. "I don't want a taxi," I told him. "I want you to call my sponsor."

He glared at me and announced angrily, "We have had enough of you. You shut up and get out of here right now or we'll lock you up and no one will ever know what happened to you."

A cold chill raced down my spine. This was the most frightening moment of my life. I knew that it would take them only a few seconds to lock me up and no one would know what had happened to Simon Estes.

I didn't stop to argue. Without running, I walked as fast as possible to the front door and found a pay phone. Soon, a car from the sponsoring organization picked me up. My hosts became very upset when I told them my story and they immediately complained to the proper authorities.

The story made the front page of the following day's newspapers. The commission demanded an apology and the police sent a formal letter saying they regretted the incident, but, according to them, "Mr. Estes' own attitude was not especially helpful." The letter went on to say, "No doubt the American police are more accustomed than our officers in dealing with the artistic temperaments of musical celebrities."

The people with whom I worked deeply regretted the entire incident. Aside from the actions of these overzealous policemen, the vast majority of those I met were wonderful caring people whom I enjoyed a great deal.

But I'll never forget the fear. I can still see that room and hear that man threaten, "No one will ever know what happened to you."

"IMPLY GRAND!"
THE NEW YORK TIMES

"SPLENDID!"
NEW YORK

"OWERFUL!"
CHICAGO TRIBUNE

"IMPOSING!"
BOSTON GLOBE

"GORGEOUS!"
WASHINGTON POST

"OUTSTAND**

LONDON T

"EXTRAORDINARY!"
BERLIN MORGENPOST

"GREAT!"
MOSCOW PRAVDA

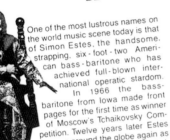

One of the most lustrous names on the world music scene today is that of Simon Estes, the handsome, strapping, six - foot - two American bass-baritone who has achieved full-blown international operatic stardom.

In 1966 the bass-baritone from Iowa made front pages for the first time as winner of Moscow's Tchaikovsky Competition. Twelve years later Estes was news around the globe again as the first male singer of his race to appear at the hallowed Richard Wagner shrine in Bayreuth, where the composer's grandson chose him for the title role of "The Flying Dutchman", a part he has since sung 23 times in 4 successive Bayreuth Festivals.

Since then Estes has been starred at virtually all of the major opera houses of the United States and Europe, performing 84 leading roles, including Wagner's King Marke and the three Wotans; all four villains of "Tales of Hoffmann"; the title roles of "Boris Godounov" and "Attila"; King Phillip in "Don Carlo", Sarastro in "The Magic Flute", Escamillo in "Carmen", Oreste in "Elektra", Pizarro in "Fidelio" and Arkel in "Pelleas et Melisande". And in January of 1982 his operatic career comes full cycle with a debut as the "Tannhäuser" Landgraf at New York's Metropolitan, where he previously brought down the house in an All-Wagner concert with Birgit Nilsson.

With a repertoire of more than 50 oratorios and symphonic works, Estes has also appeared as soloist with most of the world's leading orchestras, under conductors including Abbado, Bernstein, Boulez, Dorati, Giulini, Kubelik, Leinsdorf, Levine, Ma Mehta, Muti, Ormandy and Ozawa. Ormandy he gave the U.S. premiere Shostakovich Fourteenth Symphon with Dorati was soloist for the gala co opening the Kennedy Center. In 19 sang the title role for a historic produ of Verdi's first opera "Oberto" in Bo and in 1979 was the Pharoah for a ble revival of Rossini's "Mosè in E at La Scala.

On recordings Estes is heard in Shostakovich Fourteenth and M delssohn's "Walpurgisnacht" (Ormandy and the Philadelphi and "Judas Maccabaeus" (wit New York Handel Society) for Carlo" (with Caballé, Domingo a "Koanga" (with Sir Charles G in Haydn's "Lord Nelson Ma messe" (with Leonard Berns Philharmonic). Rachmar André Kostelanetz) ar nella" (with Pierre Bou "Oberto" for Italia; ar neo" and Monteverd for Teldec. He is als sion of "Ulisse" by Unitel. A con has given more other singer on th maxed by a 1980 THE NEW YOR ply grand'.

CARNEGIE HALL
1997–98 SEASON

Saturday Evening, February 7, 1998, at 8:00

THE COLLEGIATE CHORALE
Robert Bass, *Music Director*

Fifty-seventh Season

Giuseppe Verdi
NABUCCO
Lyrical drama in four parts

Libretto by Temistocle Solera

THE ORCHESTRA OF ST. LUKE'S
Robert Bass, *Conductor*

Characters in order of vocal appearance:

Zaccaria, a Hebrew prophet	Simon Estes
Ismaele, nephew of the King of Jerusalem	Hugh Smith
Fenena, Nabucco's daughter	Susanna Poretsky
Abigaille, a slave, believed to be the oldest daughter of Nabucco	Lauren Flanigan
Nabucco, King of Babylon	Donnie Ray Albert
Anna, Zaccaria's sister	Eileen Koyl
High Priest of Baal	Charles Austin
and devoted officer of Nabucco	Bo Song
ws, Levites, Virgins, Soldiers, Old Men, Soothsayers, Nobles	The Collegiate Chorale and the Riverside Choral Society

There will be one intermission after Part 2

ic Director's Chair for the 1997–98 season has been underwritten by a generous gift from Mrs. Edna B. Salomon.

This concert is underwritten, in part, by a generous gift from Daisy and Paul Soros.

This evening's performance is made possible, in part, by generous gifts from Susan Baker and Michael Lynch, Rose Barell, Roxanne Brandt, Edythe and Mathew Gladstein, and Francis Goelet.

Discrimination in American opera remains a serious problem. The values and attitudes my parents taught me have guided this aspect of my life, as well. Even though those in management positions in the United States have not accepted black opera singers, I kept moving ahead and built my career in Europe. I am not bitter; I do try to counter injustice factually and peacefully.

When some insist there is no prejudice in American opera, I ask them to name black males who are singing title and leading roles today. After they name a few black women, I point out that they have named practically no black males. The fact is that I am about the only black male with a major career in the opera world today. This is not because I am the first to be blessed with a great voice. I have many predecessors like William Warfield who never sang opera in the United States, and any number of young black singers with excellent talent deserve to be singing in major opera houses in this country.

It has been easier for black women than for black men to play romantic leads on stage and in movies, and the same is true in opera in this country. Perhaps a black man singing to a white woman threatens some people. My colleagues, 99% of whom are white, certainly don't object to my singing with them.

Audiences convince me they don't care about color; they care about excellent singing and first-rate acting. When I sing opera in this country, the audience response is beautiful.

Ten years ago, only twenty percent of my performances took place in my own country. That rate is slowly improving. On a larger scale, I am about the only black male performing regularly in opera anywhere in the world. Charles Kellis describes this situation as "ridiculous" and a "tragedy for younger black singers for whom Simon should be setting an example."

When young black artists ask me for help, I encourage them to keep trying to share their gift with those who want to hear it. I tell them, "You must be strong. You must endure. We have suffered all our lives, but we cannot let another barrier keep us from sharing our gifts with others."

This problem pervades the world of classical music, not just opera. Similar to sports, one can be a player but not a manager. Opera houses in this country have black ushers, janitors, elevator operators, etc., but how many blacks are in policy-making or decision-making positions? When people are deprived of sharing their gifts, that is injustice for them, and priceless irreplaceable loss for the rest of us.

Perhaps this is not racism, but it is certainly a problem with sociological dimensions. Part of my professional mission is to remove the barriers. I hope the day will come when skin color will no longer be an issue that divides.

ohn F. Kennedy Cen____ ____ g Arts

Simon Estes is an incredible artist with a magnificent instrument—his voice with its sheer power and incredible vocal technique. That he is spiritual is conveyed through his music.

Younger singers learn so much from him: voice, stage presence to name a few. It is a great honor and privilege to sing with him in Verdi's *Simon Boccanegra*.

— Kallen Esperian, Soprano

Refrain

Going home to Centerville. Rich memories and joyous reunions always mark my return trips to Centerville. In May of 1994, I enjoyed an incredible week of renewing friendships, attending special events, and participating in small-town get-togethers with great Iowa cooking!

Jerry Bowen, a CBS correspondent formerly from Centerville, devoted an entire week to filming my visit. It later aired on CBS *Sunday Morning* with Charles Kuralt. I also spoke to students. I encouraged them to keep their values, to not let anyone or anything take them away. I also urged them to say "no" to alcohol and drugs. "It is the strong person who says 'no' and the weak person who says 'yes.' Remember the hero is right inside you!"

My benefit concert for the renovation of the high school auditorium capped the week's activities. As a boy, I loved singing in that auditorium—I felt free there, I could be myself. It meant a great deal to me to show my love and support for my school, my hometown, and my many friends in this way. It was my finest Centerville concert.

I was thrilled and humbled to learn that the renovated auditorium would bear my name. I accepted this honor not for myself but as a message for all current and future students and for all African-Americans and non-African-Americans; as a message that African-Americans can achieve great things; and as a message that we have made great strides in brotherhood when an African-American can be honored in such a way.

I was extremely surprised and deeply moved to be named the first recipient of the "Distinguished Alumni Award," which recognizes Centerville graduates who have achieved unusual success. Tears stung my eyes. I couldn't speak for a few moments, but I wanted everyone to know what was in my heart and that I was still the same Simon Estes—just with a little more weight and a little less hair! Nothing equals the joy of coming home.

At the end of the concert, I remembered seeing my sister Westella being the first person to stand for an ovation after I finished singing, "Precious Lord, Take My Hand."

The joy of this benefit concert which meant so much to me was tragically interrupted later that evening by news that Westella and our cousin Constance Barnes had been killed in a car accident when driving back to Des Moines following the concert.

I am honored that the renovated Centerville High School auditorium bears my name, with this dedication inscription to welcome patrons.

When I returned to Centerville in September of 1997, I enjoyed serving as parade marshal for "Pancake Days," an annual event sponsored by local business people as a way of thanking their patrons. That visit was characterized also by my "job" flipping pancakes, a number of events featuring great Iowa food, a pick-up basketball game on the same court where I played as a young man, renewing many old friendships as well as making new ones, and a concert attended by my former high school music teacher, Don Gunderson. Barbara Bradley Cortesio, my accompanist from eighth grade at Washington Junior High through graduation from Centerville High School, was at the piano. We were often featured on this very stage where 41 years later we would once again share a local concert appearance.

While growing up in Centerville, I endured some experiences common to blacks everywhere at that time, but this community gave me a wonderful education, great friends, and helpful encouraging people. Centerville certainly has a very special place in my heart.

The values I learned there from my parents, my friends, people in my church, people in my school, and people in the community have stayed with me all these years. They continue to influence my mission in life and how I carry it out as I interact with people around the world.

Going home to Iowa. In 1996, the Des Moines City Council named its new outdoor riverfront performance pavilion "The Simon Estes Amphitheatre." I am honored that this place—which provides opportunities for all types of artists to perform as well as the community to enjoy them—bears my name.

On July 3, 1996, my home state bestowed on me the Iowa Award, its highest citizen award. During its 50-year existence, only twelve other

Veronica Scully, of Manchester, England, was the accompanist for the Simon Estes 1997–1998 Iowa Tour. It included a concert in the Centerville High School Auditorium where I was also accompanied by Barbara Bradley Cortesio, my accompanist throughout junior and senior high school.

Iowans have been recognized for their "outstanding service" and the "merit of their accomplishments in Iowa and throughout the United States." Because I love Iowa and Iowans, I felt honored and humbled to have been chosen to receive this award. During Iowa's sesquicentennial celebration concert with the Des Moines Symphony on the state capitol grounds, I accepted the award with these words:

"First, I thank God because God is Love. If it weren't for God, I wouldn't be who I am today. I feel very blessed in having been born in Iowa to Ruth Estes who is here tonight and to Simon Estes who is now in heaven and whose spirit is here with us. I'm grateful for parents and sisters and a brother who loved me and helped me become the individual I am today. I do not take the credit myself because when something is being built, many individuals are involved in building that person or structure or that nation. Many people—my schoolteachers in Centerville, Iowa, religious leaders, even political leaders—[helped] form my character, my values, and my principles. I am the luckiest man, not only in Iowa but in the world, to have been born here. I hope Iowa continues to lead this country and the world to become closer together as brothers and sisters."

My 1997–1998 Iowa tour allowed me to give back to my home state some of what it and its citizens have given to me over the years. To come home to Iowa as a professional singer and share with these people the gift God gave me is so touching and meaningful. I don't have words to explain what an honor, joy, and privilege it is to sing for as many Iowans as I possibly can.

Going home to Africa. Early in 1995 something inside me said, "Make the African trip." The Nico Opera house in Cape Town, South Africa, asked me to perform the title role in Verdi's opera *Nabucco*. For 20 years, South African opera management encouraged me to perform there; I refused because of apartheid. But apartheid had ended, South Africans—75% of whom are black—were free, Nelson Mandela served as President, and I had the opportunity to be the first black opera singer in a new Cape Town, South Africa.

I always feel a responsibility to each audience, but in South Africa, I strongly felt additional responsibilities. To my black South African brothers and sisters, I owed my best as a response to their joy that I was there and as an encouragement to the new opportunities that were opening for them. To my white brothers and sisters who showed courage in issuing the invitation for me to perform, I wanted to offer the same: only my best.

I went as an American ambassador and as a catalyst, especially for black South Africans. I wanted my presence to help their transition into music and opera. Sunday afternoon and evening, I conducted master classes for talented young singers with great potential.

Even though obstacles remain in their country as well as in my own, I encouraged them that they can now move into these new areas of music and opera.

Archbishop Desmond Tutu invited me to sing for the Sunday morning service at the Cathedral Church of St. George. This church has always been known as a place of dissent and is considered the birthplace of freedom for the new South Africa. What more appropriate song for me to sing than the negro spiritual "Let My People Go."

We say German American, Italian American, Irish American, etc., but until the last few years no one said African American. When we did acknowledge ourselves as African, it was embarrassing. How good it felt to be an African American in Africa despite the astounding contrast between white and black areas.

When I first stepped off the plane and into the terminal in Cape Town, a young black South African choir sang what sounded to me like a native song. I thought, "What a clever tradition, singing to welcome the passengers as they enter the airport terminal!" I stopped to listen to these outstanding voices and it was then that I heard my name interwoven in the young people's song. I was both startled and pleased.

A lady, who I later learned was the choir director, approached me. "Simon Estes, welcome home and we love you."

For the rest of my life, I will never forget that feeling when she spoke those words: "Welcome to your Motherland." To be in this country where blacks are the majority was a new phenomenon. Never before had I experienced that strong sensation of pride and the feeling of really being home. With a lump in my throat, I said, "For the first time in my life, I know where my roots are. Thank you. I have never been home before. I am African and American. Today I feel I know who this African-American truly is."

Wanting to repay the students' kindness, I visited their school. Here in the worst possible living conditions, I found a high school choir with the most amazing voices and a pure tone. Led by Nolufefe Mtshabe, the Masiyile High School chorus was winning competitions in South Africa. The school did not own a pitch pipe or a piano, but they made beautiful music. Before I left, I bought the school a piano, taught them how to care for it, and promised to return.

When I left South Africa, the students came to the airport to thank me for visiting this part of the world and their school. A different Simon Estes left South Africa than the one who had arrived a few days before. I would return.

My second trip to the Motherland. South Africa beckoned me again and in the spring of 1996, groups from Des Moines, Iowa, and Tulsa, Oklahoma, accompanied me. They brought boxes and boxes of clothing, school supplies, cash, and letters from students of all ages for the Masiyile High students, along with their good will. And thanks to one generous young Iowan, a musical bonus.

While in Gowrie, Iowa, for a concert, I was enjoying breakfast in a cafe when I received a request to speak to students at the local high school. Since talking to students is one of my favorite activities, I instantly agreed.

As the students and I talked in the high school music room, I recounted the needs of Masiyile High School students. The African students were interested in forming a band, but of course they had no instruments or money to buy them.

Jessica Grell, a Prairie Valley High School senior, offered to donate her clarinet. "Will you take it to that high school for me?"

Overwhelmed by her generosity, I could barely finish my talk. With her one gift, this young lady unleashed a torrent of donations.

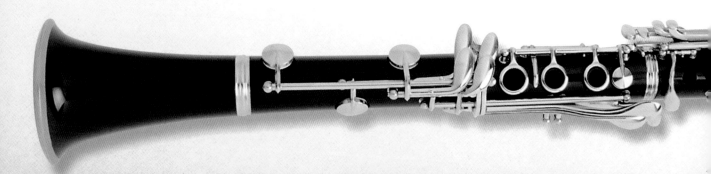

That next Sunday when I performed with the Des Moines Symphony, Jessica presented her clarinet to me during the intermission. Band director Alan Greiner and vocal director Mary Egger of Prairie Valley joined us on stage. I had heard rumors that more instruments were coming, but when Alan pointed to our right and out came 52 instruments, it was like a dream!

In just a few days, people at that small school contacted other communities and the drive for instruments was under way. Music stores, music publishing companies, Pak Mail, United Parcel Service, and Swiss Air—to name a few—made sure the musical instruments arrived in Cape Town a few weeks later.

Despite their being on holiday during my later trip to Cape Town, the Masiyile High students and parents held a tea and concert for the people from Des Moines and Tulsa. On the tea table as a centerpiece was Jessica Grell's clarinet, the symbol of my native state's generosity.

In March, several other American musicians traveled with me to Cape Town to perform *Porgy and Bess* with the Opera. This group included Willy Anthony Waters, Cynthia Clarey, James Butler, and Ronald T. Smith.

Residents of the area combined with us to form the predominently all-black cast.

In addition to a concert in Durban, I joined South African soprano Marita Napier and the Cape Philharmonic Orchestra for a Verdi and Wagner concert.

On Good Friday, April 7, 1996, Archbishop Desmond Tutu invited me to sing at his noontime service in the Cathedral of St. George. What an honor! At his very moving and spiritual service, I sang "Thus Saith the Lord" from the *Messiah*. The next day, the Archbishop and I met to discuss a variety of topics regarding the new South Africa. My trips to South Africa have been extremely fulfilling. That area needs so much, and we must all help them prosper in any way we can. I look forward to my next trip to that beautiful country and its beautiful people.

Highlights of my second trip to South Africa were the presentation of musical instruments, including the clarinet donated by Jessica Grell, to Masiyile High school students and Archbishop Desmond Tutu's invitation to sing at the Cathedral Church of St. George.

Wagner
LE VAISSEAU FANTÔME

Simon Estes
Lisbeth Balslev

Salminen · Schunk · Schlemm · Clark

Bayreuther Festspiele
Woldemar Nelsson

2 Compact Discs 416 300-2
3 LP 416 300-1   3 MC 416 300-4

Practice and Performance

Everyone thinks opera singers lead glamorous lives. That is true to some extent, but endless hours of practice and preparation make up the other side of the coin. As I travel from country to country and continent to continent, the time I spend alone in hotel rooms and strange towns without my family and friends often becomes tiresome. On occasion, I have meals with peers, but I spend most of my time in my hotel room reading, watching TV, thinking, and meditating.

It's always a little troubling to realize how much I depend on my voice. Because it is my meal ticket, I have to be careful and coddle it. If I damage my vocal cords, my career as a singer will end.

Do I sing in the shower? No, I do not, but I do take showers! Most people who sing for a living sing only at rehearsals, performances, and for special friends or events. Occasionally someone asks me to "sing a little something." I always avoid doing so, not because I think I'm the star who only sings for money, but because I must protect my voice. At a social function, I wouldn't ask my doctor to whip out his stethoscope and listen to my heart or ask my dentist to check a loose filling. Singers are professionals, too.

The basics of my career are always a curious point for people. When do I practice? Where do I practice? How long do I practice? How do I memorize an opera or pieces for a concert? How is a recording made?

I don't practice unless it's necessary. (Sorry, mothers of would-be musicians who stress practice!) I've been singing for more than 30 years, so I have already put in extensive practice time. When I am called on to sing one of the many roles I have memorized, I just review the music.

I am able to memorize most operas in two weeks. Verdi operas take only one week because most of his works are not complicated. I learned Verdi's *Nabucco* with eight hours of piano rehearsals. Wagner's *Die Walküre*, which is more complicated, took longer.

I memorize music and words together. I am thankful I was blessed with a nearly photographic memory. After I've studied the music, I close my eyes and see the words, notes, and music as they appear in the score. I even remember where a particular word or note is located on a page.

If I memorize an opera quickly, in four days for example, and only sing a few performances, I forget most of it.

If I learn an opera quickly and sing ten performances, I remember almost everything. If I have a longer time to memorize, perhaps a month, and then do ten performances, I almost never forget it.

Generally speaking, the principals in a new opera production devote four to six weeks to staging rehearsals. Before rehearsals begin, the stage director presents his/her concept of the opera and interpretation of the story, and how to portray the characters.

Many stage directors encourage artists to share their own ideas because it then becomes a richer and more diversified performance. In rehearsal, I bring my interpretation of the role within the stage director's concept. Consistent with the

Simon Estes is the consummate artist. He has been generously endowed with creative talent and he has persisted with exquisite discipline in honing and polishing that talent. The gifts of the artist remind us of the love of the Creator. Thank you Simon Estes.

— Dr. Maya Angelou, Beloved poet, author, and teacher

job responsibilities, he adds suggestions and we all work together.

During the last two weeks before the first performance, singers concentrate on the music and staging. Staging is practicing our movements on stage: where we stand, how we stand, to whom we sing at a particular time. Woe to the hero who sings a love song to the wrong lady because he's standing where he shouldn't be!

Then the whole cast meets with the conductor while he goes through the entire score, explaining how he wants the opera interpreted musically. Next, the singers have a "hauptprobe" or general rehearsal with the conductor, piano, costumes, makeup, and lighting. Finally, the pre-dress rehearsal and the dress rehearsal come one or two days before the performance.

Concerts and recitals follow a somewhat different path from operas. Most often, only a soloist and an accompanist perform in recitals. Because recitals are often booked a year in advance, I have time to think about that performance. Notice I didn't say I *work* on the performance for a year. I just think about it until a few weeks before the performance, knowing that I will sing from memory rather than printed music. My accompanist and I run through the music together one or two days before the performance, but he or she usually wants the music much earlier. The day before a recital, my accompanist and I check out the acoustics and the lighting. The lighting is especially important because the accompanist must be able to see the music, and I don't like singing to darkened concert halls where I can't see the people and communicate with them. If a spotlight is on me, I feel as if I'm singing to myself. I am there to sing for that audience and I want to see them.

In Europe's smaller halls, I can see more people. Sometimes I look right at one individual and I feel I'm in touch with him or her.

Concerts, on the other hand, usually involve one or more soloists—either singers or instrumentalists or both—and an orchestra. Singers arrive three days before an orchestra date. If the concert is on Saturday, a piano rehearsal is held on Thursday morning and an orchestra rehearsal on Thursday night. Friday follows the same schedule. On the day of the performance, singers conserve their voices by trying not to talk too much.

When I was younger, I arrived at the hall 10 or 15 minutes before a concert or recital performance. Now that I'm "more mature" (a nice phrase for "older"), I arrive an hour early.

In most concerts, the singer does not use music during the performance; however, there are exceptions. With modern music instead of the old masters, the music comes in handy. For some works like the *Messiah* or a Beethoven work, the artist can choose whether to sing from memory or music.

Recording sessions provide fewer choices because they are more complex than concerts or recitals. The first step involves an orchestra rehearsal and a balance test. At the recording studio, the artist stands in front of the microphone and sings a few phrases while the orchestra plays a few bars. The engineers assess the two while deciding how close the singer will stand to the mike. Because a singer's volume ranges from very soft (*sotto voce*) to very loud (*fortissimo*), all levels must be tested. The vocalist sings a selection from an aria after which he, the conductor, and the producer go to the control room for a listen-back. They evaluate any changes necessary in the singer's position and voice. Were any notes flat or sharp? Too loud?

Modern technology greatly enhances the making of a recording. A note sung flat can be deleted and replaced with the correct note. If a word is mispronounced, the singer re-records that one word or a few bars and the technician inserts the correct word. If a portion of a song is

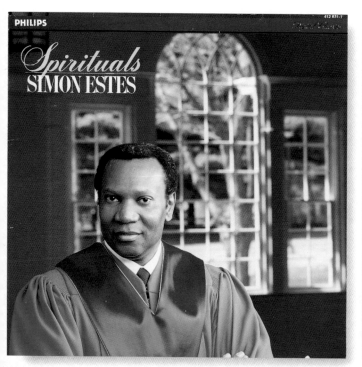

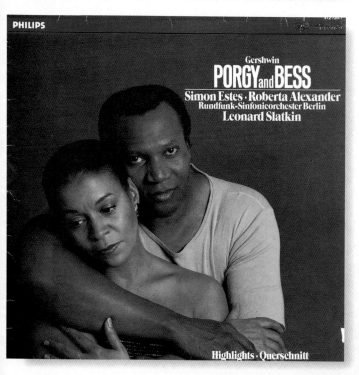

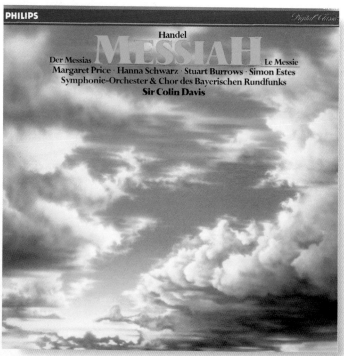

For various reasons, recording sessions make more demands and put more pressure on a singer than concerts or recitals. I always give 110% and I'm always prepared for every concert, recital, recording, or opera performance...just like my high school basketball coach taught me.

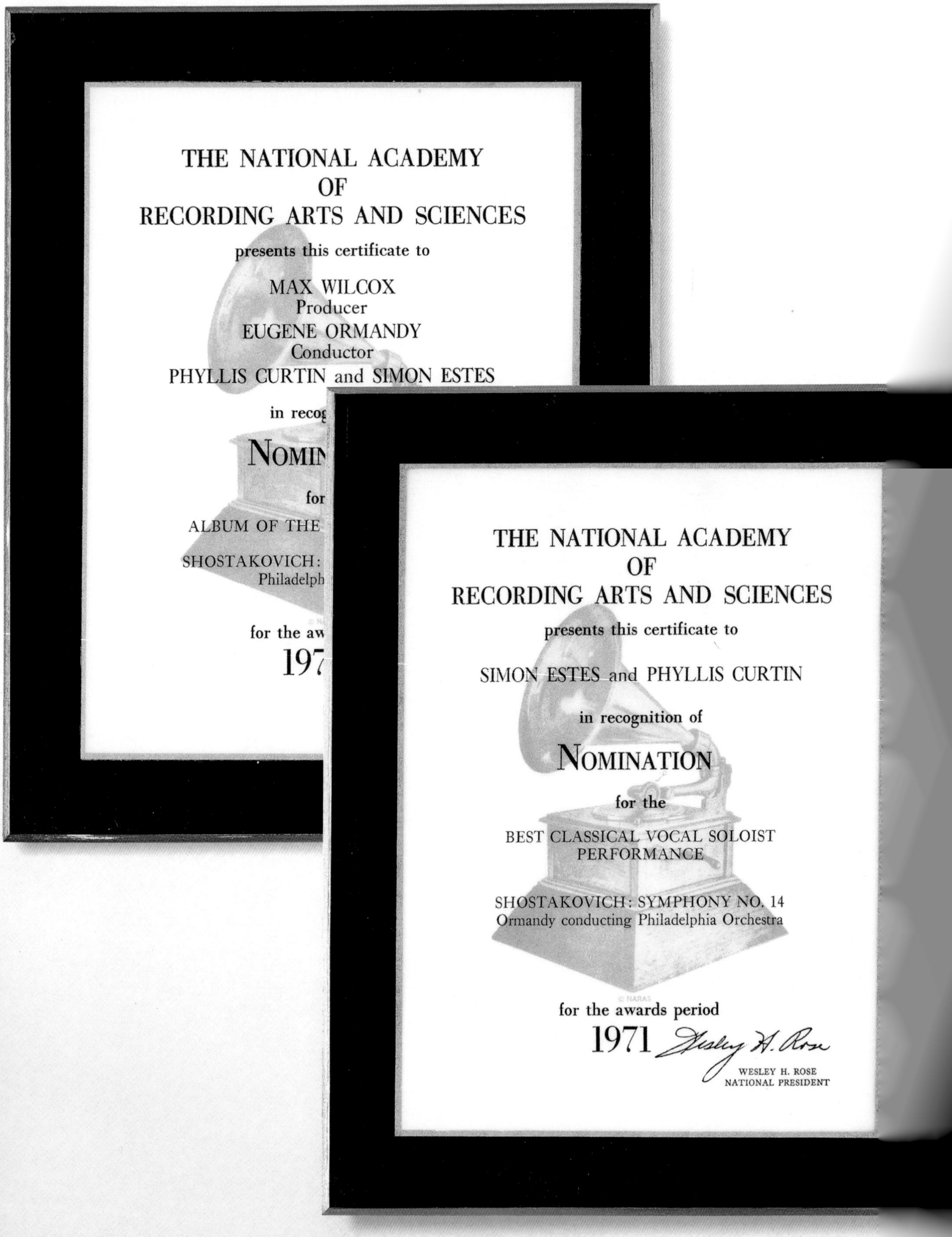

**THE NATIONAL ACADEMY
OF
RECORDING ARTS AND SCIENCES**

presents this certificate to

MAX WILCOX
Producer
EUGENE ORMANDY
Conductor
PHYLLIS CURTIN and SIMON ESTES

in recog

NOMIN

for

ALBUM OF THE

SHOSTAKOVICH:
Philadelph

for the aw

197

**THE NATIONAL ACADEMY
OF
RECORDING ARTS AND SCIENCES**

presents this certificate to

SIMON ESTES and PHYLLIS CURTIN

in recognition of

NOMINATION

for the

BEST CLASSICAL VOCAL SOLOIST
PERFORMANCE

SHOSTAKOVICH: SYMPHONY NO. 14
Ormandy conducting Philadelphia Orchestra

for the awards period
1971

WESLEY H. ROSE
NATIONAL PRESIDENT

not right, the singer repeats it and the sound engineer mixes one or two of these sections to make a complete song.

Once in a while, I sing a whole song through without any major mistakes. After all this hard work, each song takes only about five minutes to play. If I am to record a total of 16 songs, we work on only three or four each day, two hours in the morning and two hours in the afternoon. Recording an entire opera usually takes a week or ten days.

If the recording takes place in an opera house, outside noise can be a problem. To avoid traffic sounds or sirens that can ruin a recording, we schedule the session during a quiet time of day. We also consider proper lighting and proper ventilation.

Sensitive microphones pick up the sound of air blowing from a ventilator. Sometimes old structures creak, and any section of the recording with those noises must be redone. For various reasons, recording sessions make more demands and put more pressure on a singer than concerts or recitals.

After the recording is completed, it must be mixed and balanced. Then the principals are called in to listen to the finished product and to discuss whether the recording is satisfactory. Usually, only famous stars and powerful conductors decide if the tape or disk is released.

In music, we often say you sing on the interest, not the principal. You always need to keep a little something in reserve.

However, I always give 110% and am always prepared for every concert, recital, recording, or opera performance…just like my high school basketball coach taught me.

A gift from God. Students sometimes wonder, "Right before you perform, what's going through your mind?"

I'm not a nervous, shaky performer. I'm excited about singing! I'm kind of like a race horse that can't wait for the gate to open and the race

to start. I'm thinking about what I'm going to perform. I'm grateful, I look forward to singing, and I am excited about the performance.

Students often ask if I am a perfectionist. Yes, I strive for perfection, but perfection is a relative term. It depends upon one's ability. If a person prepares and performs to the best of his ability, he has worked a great degree towards perfection. I strive towards perfection, but I don't think we as human beings can ever attain it. That does not mean we should not try with every fiber of energy and talent and gift we have.

I've been told that something in my voice touches the hearts of my audiences. After a concert, people come backstage and often tell me that a particular song moved them, sometimes to tears. I attribute that ability to God. He allows me to communicate my emotions to my listeners through a special timbre in my voice. That ability has contributed to my success more than anything else.

People ask me, "You're very religious, aren't you?" I am.

When people ask that question, I sometimes answer with another: "Why do you ask?"

A typical response is, "Something very special came through your singing. When I heard it, I felt you have a close relationship with God."

My family was deeply religious and I am grateful for that foundation. God was the great constant in our lives, the one place we turned for solace and answers. With a loving Father, our lives were a bit easier.

Before I sing, I always bow my head and thank God for my talent. I firmly believe my voice is a gift from Him.

All talents, whether you're a physician, painter, or athlete, are gifts God has given. In gratitude to Him, we need to develop them as best we can.

Our hard work, study, good choices, and sacrifices can improve our gifts, but we should always remember that the basic talent comes from God.

MACBETH
OPERNHAUS ZÜRICH

I love playing Macbeth from
Verdi's opera adaptation. I find
this long baritone role rewarding.

The role with which I have been identified most frequently is Wagner's Flying Dutchman.

DER FLIEGENDE **Holländer**

ESTES + DUTCHMAN = "SOVEREIGN AUTHORITY"

HAMBURG DIE ZEIT

THE NEW YORK TIMES

BAYREUTH, West Germany, July 26 (AP)—Simon Estes won acclaim last night in "The Flying Dutchman" at the opening of the 1978 Bayreuth Festival.

The 40-year-old bass-baritone from Centerville, Iowa received thunderous applause from a capacity crowd.

MUNICH MERKUR

...Simon Estes...impressed with the extraordinary projective power and endurance of his bass-baritone. His splendid, agile playing depicted a Hollander tormented to the point of despair and fanatically groping for salvation.

INTERNATIONAL HERALD TRIBUNE

...a splendidly rich-voiced Dutchman, soaringly defiant rather than doom-laden.

NUREMBERG NACHRICHTEN

With the singer-actor Simon Estes, a star was born. He is superior to all his predecessors in the role.

HAMBURG ABENDBLATT

It was tremendously fascinating to observe how the black giant Simon Estes identified with his role and its demonic conception. This was a complete triumph from start to finish...

VIENNA ZEITUNG

As interpreter of the title role, Simon Estes offered a brilliant performance. His voice is a bit reminiscent of the voice of George London at its best. It is voluminous and at the same time elegant in timbre.

VIENNA NEUE KRONENZEITUNG

A grandiose performance from Simon Estes who also offered distinctly clear diction which no German singer today can match.

STUTTGART NACHRICHTEN

Simon Estes, the first male negro singer in the 102 year history of Bayreuth, is ideally cast from appearance and voice. He portrays the inner strife of this figure through vocal versatility and nuances.

BERLIN TAGESSPIEGEL

Simon Estes sings the Monologue in such truly stirring manner that I had to fight against my emotions although I have been hardened for some time in the business of criticism. Estes preserved the artistic character of his performance by staying away from cheap sentimentality. The musical declamation as well as the dramatic portrayal were equally refined, and his baritone voice surmounted the whole at the end through unprecedented and beautiful sounding reserves according to the wishes of the composer: "Here the nobility of expression must be at its highest point."

Although he is power-hungry, the character of Boris Godunov possesses some redeeming qualities as a father. The role is very demanding and is sung in Russian.

I consider "Don Carlo" to be Verdi's best opera,
with each character performing a beautiful
and demanding aria or duet.

I immerse myself in a role to the extent that I become that character, but only on stage. When I walk into my dressing room and remove my makeup and costume, the role comes off, too. I am Simon Estes, not Attila or Porgy to Roberta Alexander's Bess or any of the evil personalities from the "Tales of Hoffman."

Neither am I Scarpia from "Tosca," nor Saul, nor am I Amonasro from "Aida." I am the kid from Centerville who never dreamed he'd get farther east than Chicago.

The role of Jochanaan in "salome" holds spiritual significance for me because he is a messenger of God. The beautiful Ljuba Kazarnovskaya portrayed salome in the 1996 Canadian Opera Company production.

Singing in the title role of Boccanegra—his 100th role—Mr. Estes displays a stellar talent that for too long has remained hidden from American audiences. Mr. Estes turned in one of the most powerful and authoritative performances we have seen in recent years at the [Kennedy Center] Opera House.

— T. L. Ponick,
The Washington Times

Placido Domingo asked me to portray the title role of Simon Boccanegra for the Washington Opera Company at the Kennedy Center in Washington, D.C.

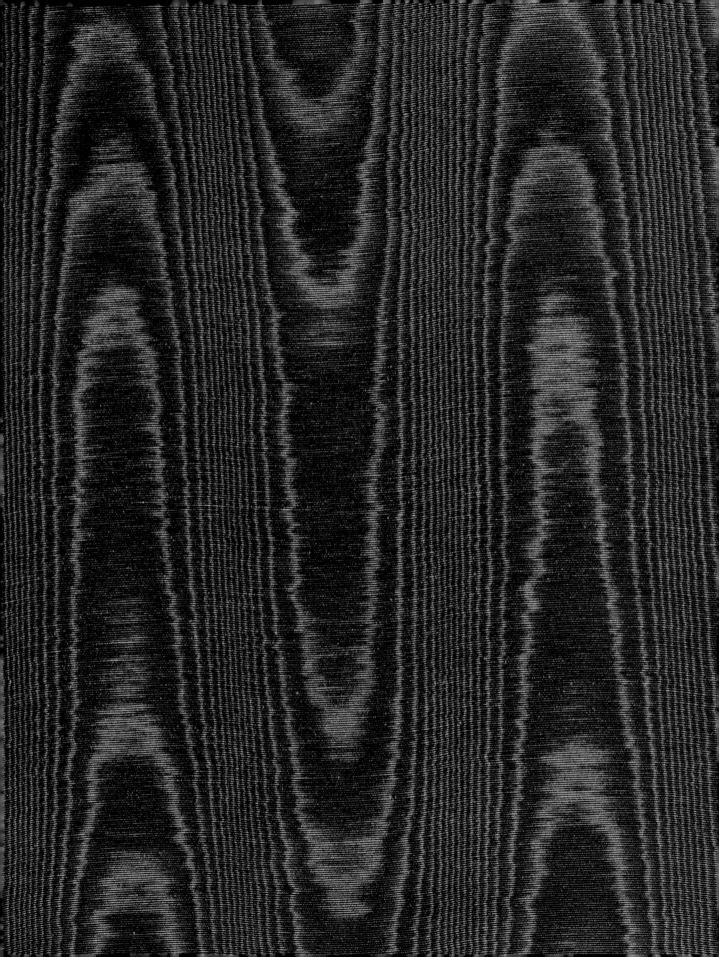

CHAPTER THREE

The Mission

We are put on earth for two reasons: to serve God and to serve others. The ways in which we do so are shaped by our personal experiences, values we grow up learning, professional experiences, opportunities and needs we become aware of, and how we use our positions, resources, and gifts to make a difference. For me, singing has become a way to accomplish larger purposes.

I know what it is like to be poor, to struggle financially to get through college, and to struggle professionally because of the color of my skin. During the years when I had absolutely no money, I knew that if I were ever blessed, I wanted to help people—especially children. Because slavery broke our family chain, I know the loss that accompanies brokenness and separation. It has taught me that through education, shared cultural experiences, and improved understanding, we not only can but we must forge peaceful new links among our one human race.

We must continually work to create a world in which all young people are recognized for their abilities, encouraged to develop them, and then appreciated when they share those gifts and talents.

God gave me the gift of an exceptional voice. When I put it to use for His glory, I can also use the benefits to help others. I'm just one

My friend General Colin Powell and I both care deeply about helping children.

person—one person in a big, huge world—but I think all of us have to do our part to make the world a better place and to help children. It takes extra time and it takes extra energy, but it must be done.

I try to act "ambassadorial" everywhere I go. The values I try to model are those my parents modeled for me: faith, honesty, loyalty, hard work, patience, determination, humility, love, and peacefulness. My career has provided wonderful learning experiences for me as I have traveled around the world. These experiences reveal the needs of children and young people as well as ways to focus on educational, health, and talent development areas.

As my career has expanded, so have my horizons. I am in a position to help others, and I find that so gratifying. My career has brought me in contact with world leaders and other outstanding people. I am very humbled by these experiences. They are the reason I feel at home in the world.

In the summer of 1998, I was privileged to sing at a conference on volunteerism in which retired General Colin Powell was the featured speaker. He has many life experiences similar to mine, and shares my desire to help young people. Through General Powell's *Alliance for Youth*, he has been a role model and mentor for thousands of deserving young people.

Foundations and Scholarships

The Simon Estes Educational Foundation, Inc. was created in 1983 when I performed with the Tulsa Opera. A group of Tulsans met with me to discuss our mutual concern about promising area high school seniors who faced financial difficulty in attending college. As a non-profit organization, we provide financial assistance and promote educational opportunities in any discipline. A separate endowment trust fund insures that donated monies are permanently invested. Only income earned on the donations can be spent, and the only allowed expenditure is for scholarships.

Students in protected classes are given special consideration, but all applicants are eligible (regardless of race, religion, gender, or ethnic origin) if they meet certain qualifications:

financial need, scholastic achievement, clearly defined motivation for pursuing higher education, maturity and purpose appropriate to the demands of higher education, and a strong personal sense of values.

During the past 15 years, this Foundation has generated over one million dollars in grants and commitments for scholarships. Individuals, corporations, and colleges and universities contribute outright donations, summer jobs, matching funds, etc. I donate annual concert proceeds.

This merit-based scholarship provides $10,000 per student over a four-year period to be applied to tuition, books, and fees. A similar Junior College Scholarship offers $2,000 per student over a two-year period. Two-thirds of

THE SIMON ESTES EDUCATIONAL FOUNDATION, INC.

Not only does my mother pay for bills, but she also pays for hospital bills from my father's accident, and my older sister's schooling. Currently, my sister is paying half of her tuition, and the government is paying for the other half.

I am actively involved in my school and my community. I have served various student government offices, and received numerous academic and leadership honors. I have put my life in the hands of God, and have asked him to guide me down the correct paths. I have al... ...ed to be the best in everything, and my grades and a...

I am not asking you to pity ... but, I am only stating the truth ...

Please consider my application, ...

I know that there will be other ...

but I am asking to please revie... ...

Sincerely,

Phuong-Chi T. Duong

Jayne L. Reed, a founder of the The Simon Estes Educational Foundation in Tulsa, Oklahoma, receives inspiring scholarship application letters, such as the one from Phuong-Chi T. Duong who is now studying at Oklahoma State University.

Dwight Eskew, another Simon Estes Educational Foundation scholarship recipient, is a student at Morehouse College in Atlanta and plans to become a neurosurgeon.

each award is in the form of a grant; one-third is a loan which recipients must pay back for several reasons. First, I believe students shouldn't get something for nothing. Second, they need to be fully committed to their education. Third, in repaying their loan, they invest in the future of still more young people. We have a 100% repayment record, and we currently award 12 scholarships each year.

To date, the Foundation has assisted 148 students who have attended prestigious colleges and universities in this country, who have participated in international study programs, and who are now professionals. They are our greatest endorsement. They get to see their dreams come true, and we get to watch. As we help young people develop their gifts and learn to share them, the community is strengthened.

Dwight Eskew, a scholarship recipient, is a junior at Morehouse College in Atlanta and plans to become a neurosurgeon.

Growing up was rough, with burglaries and fights common-place. Dwight's worst fear while he was growing up was that he would be kidnapped. He never knew his father; his step-father disappeared by the time Dwight was in fifth grade; his mother left a few years after that. Only one of his siblings did not drift away.

When he was 12 or 13 years old, Dwight read the book *Gifted Hands* by Dr. Ben Carson and knew he too wanted to be a neurosurgeon. After a time of "acting up a lot," as Dwight described it, he did well in school, was recognized for his good work, and he "got addicted to that praise."

He struggles semester to semester raising enough money to continue his education. He works while he is at Morehouse, and last summer break, he worked 78 hours a week. He does very well in school, earning all A's and B's. Dwight encourages others to keep trying and to know that "God always helps out."

Phuong-Chi T. Doung, another scholarship recipient, says that "From the day of my birth, I knew that I was in God's hands." Her parents were Indonesian boat people. After months of traveling and suffering from malnutrition, her mother contracted malaria, which she passed on to Chi at birth. It was feared that neither she nor her mother would live. They were saved by Christian missionaries and nurtured to health.

Now it is her parents who are ill. When Chi

was a high school junior, her father suffered a severe brain hemorrhage, leaving him permanently disabled. Her mother, suffering with the Hepatitis-C virus, continues to work in spite of her illness. Chi has great love and respect for her parents who provided her with the best of love and care. Chi has been an excellent student with musical and leadership abilities. She is currently a sophomore at Oklahoma State University majoring in Health Science, Communication Sciences and Disorders.

I consider it an honor to be able to help such worthy young people. With their abilities and positive attitudes, they will make a difference in the world. Education sets them free and benefits all of us.

The Iowa Arts Council Scholarship for the Arts. The purpose of this program is to "encourage the development of outstanding high school seniors who excel in the arts and who have enrolled in educational programs leading to careers in the arts." Each year, up to five $1000 scholarships may be awarded. Monies can be used for tuition at the Iowa college or university in which the student is enrolled. Eligibility requirements specify that applicants must be graduates of an Iowa high school; demonstrate ability in the area of visual art, music, dance, theater, or literature; and be accepted as a full-time undergraduate at an accredited Iowa college or

university in one or more of the areas listed above. The selection committee also considers the applicants' career goals.

In conjunction with serving as spokesperson for Governor Branstad's Iowa Homecoming '86, I performed a benefit concert to provide the initial funds for this program which encourages young people to remain in Iowa after graduation.

The Simon and Westella Estes Scholarship Fund. This scholarship originally bore only my name, but after my sister's death following the Centerville concert in 1994, it meant a great deal to me and our family to add her name. This fund provided one scholarship per year to a graduating Centerville High School student from its inception in 1983 until 1991. Since 1992, we have increased the award to two recipients per year.

The scholarships are based on academic achievement, activities, and need, and are available to those attending either four-year or

My strong support staff includes Gudrun Rohrbach, Personal Management; and Margarita Reich, Ambassadress of the Simon Estes International Foundation for Children.

community colleges. Although funds could be awarded to students interested in the fine arts, this is not a requirement.

The Simon Estes International Foundation for Children was established in Switzerland in 1993. I believe that every child has the God-given right to adequate nourishment, health, and education. Millions of children are denied this right. That is why I established this foundation. It exists to "offer support wherever and whenever medical care or educational resources are otherwise inadequate."

I could hardly believe it when I learned that in all of Switzerland, there were only two sterile units to treat children undergoing bone marrow transplants and that there was even a waiting list. I decided immediately to help. We organized a benefit concert in Zurich to raise money for a third sterile unit and additional nurses in the Zurich Children's Hospital. Children with leukemia and various genetic disorders sometimes require bone marrow transplants. Afterwards, they need to remain in sterile surroundings and be monitored 24 hours a

Unsere Regenbogen Kinder

day for several weeks or even months, depending on how quickly they recover from the procedure. Our efforts help many more children survive.

In Bulgaria from 1995 to 1998, we sponsored a campaign to protect children against a congenital thyroid disorder that results in severe brain damage. Funding for both of these projects came from charity concerts and generous voluntary contributions. It has been thrilling and gratifying to see the good that occurs when volunteers and donors work hand-in-hand for the common good of disadvantaged children. Our logo is a child's handprint, representing our desire to "lend a hand" wherever we possibly can. We have three aims: to enable children to live to their full potential, to ensure that a growing number of children are provided with a better start to their lives, and to enable children to grow by providing them with a worthwhile reality. With the projects we have completed so far, we have extended a helping hand to a small number of children. Our goal is to increase this number.

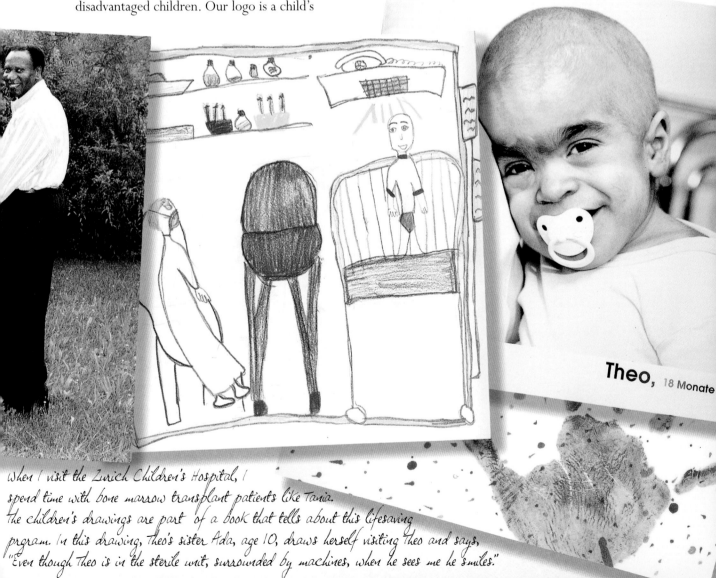

Theo, 18 Monate

When I visit the Zurich Children's Hospital, I spend time with bone marrow transplant patients like Tania. The children's drawings are part of a book that tells about this lifesaving program. In this drawing, Theo's sister Ada, age 10, draws herself visiting Theo and says, "Even though Theo is in the sterile unit, surrounded by machines, when he sees me he smiles."

The Simon Estes Fund at the University of Iowa. Initial monies for this fund came from my donation of proceeds from a recording I made with the University of Iowa Symphony Orchestra (James Dixon, Conductor). From time to time, I have made additional donations, such as the profits from a recent Iowa City concert. Funds are dispersed at the discretion of the director of music programs at the University and are administered through the UI Foundation. That person might, for instance, make capital purchases for items not covered by the Iowa Board of Regents which governs the University. He/she might also use funds to help a struggling student (I know the part well!) who is already enrolled in a program of study in the music school.

In addition to assistance available through scholarships, I have provided more direct support to several students. There are a number of young black singers on the horizon whom I expect to make great strides in this area. I hope the doors will be open for them to share their gifts.

Two of these black singers, Bongani Tembe and his wife Linda Bukhosini, are from South Africa. In 1988, a lady mentioned their singing talent to friends in Switzerland, who in turn told me about them. They auditioned for me in Switzerland. They impressed me so much that I called Charles Kellis at The Juilliard School of Music to tell him I was sending two special students his way. Several people donated funds to them, and the couple recently graduated from The Juilliard School with their bachelors and masters degrees.

They are the first black South Africans to graduate from The Juilliard School, and they have returned to their home. Mr. Tembe holds the position of deputy director for the professional Natal Philharmonic Orchestra in Durban. Linda serves as corporate affairs executive for Durban's performing arts council. Both are pursuing their careers in opera.

Another student I have helped is Michele Crider, formerly a student at the University of Iowa. Michele now has a well-established career in Europe and made her Metropolitan Opera debut this past spring. Several years ago, I invited Michele to come to Iowa City and sing with me—a concert that was very successful. We just sang together recently in a European production of *Aida*.

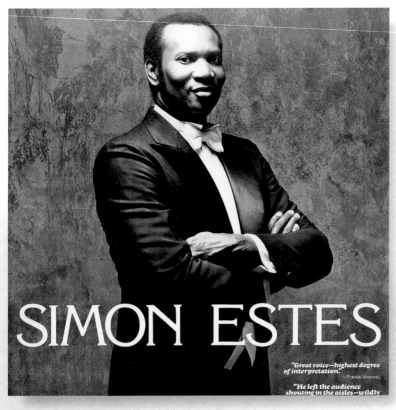

"Great voice—highest degree of interpretation."
—Pravda (Moscow)

"He left the audience shouting in the aisles—wildly

Proceeds from this album established the Simon Estes Fund at the University of Iowa.

A few years ago, I heard James Tolksdorf, a young German bass. He had an excellent voice but needed additional training. I sent him to Charles Kellis, who has been working with him for just over a year. He has made great improvement, and both Mr. Kellis and I hope he has a successful career.

I also had the opportunity to hear Abel Motsoadi, a bass from South Africa, who has a great talent. He won a prize in the Singer of the World contest in Wales. With Mr. Kellis, he's made marked progress in the two and a half years they have been working together. We expect him to embark on a great career.

I enjoy leading master classes with the world's most promising young singers. In these sessions, I listen to the students and try to advise them. I answer their questions, share my experiences, and tell them what I have learned about singing during my career. Because I have sung with so many opera companies and con-ductors, I try to steer these students in the right direction.

In these classes I tell students their roads will not be easy. I suggest contacts, and I write letters of recommendation, but they must make up their minds that they are going to work to be the best vocally.

Wherever I give a concert, I try to find an opportunity to talk with area students. I want children to see that they can achieve success through hard work, regardless of their color.

Abel Motsoadi, the student; Simon Estes, the student turned mentor, and our instructor and friend, Mr. Charles Kellis

Students ask sometimes what I think causes racism. A song from the musical *South Pacific* says we have to be carefully taught to hate the people our relatives hate. Racism is a lack of understanding not only about other people but also about other cultures and other ideas. I believe in one race, the human race.

I tell students the values essential for success in this world are honesty, dedication, respect, forgiveness, and discipline. Many would leave out "forgiveness," but one of the greatest gifts is the capacity and ability to forgive and put it into action. Then there is no place for bitterness or hatred.

[Simon] is our mentor, but he is also our friend. He has taken much more of an interest in us than a teacher-stu-dent relationship.

— Bongani Tembe &
Linda Bukhosini

Being able to make a difference in South Africa is a dream come true, but so much remains to be done.

My greatest talent is in sharing the honor and opportunity to love others.

Although ability is important, discipline and a desire to learn and achieve are important, also. Education is the solution to many of our problems today. Music also enables us to overcome most barriers put up by man. I explain to students that this combination of sounds, notes, and words touches hearts and makes us feel.

Music is one of mankind's greatest and oldest gifts and is a wonderful avenue for peace.

In every class, I tell students that I get a tremendous amount of strength and courage from God. I explain that God is love and love is God. My message is that we are all God's children even though we might have different ethnic backgrounds. As such, we are put on the earth to serve God and care for one another.

South Africa

During my first trip to South Africa in 1995, I saw living conditions that were abominable. As I flew in, I glanced down from the airplane and could barely believe my eyes. I was shocked by the shantytowns that have sprung up around Cape Town in recent years. Local officials believe 400,000 people live in these ramshackle communities just ten miles from the refined hotels and shops of Cape Town. The contrast between the black communities and white South African communities is astounding.

As soon as I was able, I visited one of these "squatters' camps." I was stunned. As I walked among the shacks and visited the terribly crowded schools nearby, I was overwhelmed by living conditions that were the worst I have ever seen.

Thousands of blacks exist in shacks built with pieces of tin, old boards, anything they can find and bring home. They have no electricity or running water. Garbage piles up right outside their doors. Entire families live in a confined space often not bigger than 15' x 16'. A few portable toilets set up just outside the commu-

nity serve the entire population. Some children have no parents but reside in the shanties alone. Food is scarce, and it is not unusual for a student to faint from hunger while at school.

These are dangerous places to live. During our visit, some taxi and bus drivers refused to enter Khayelitsha Township. At Masiyile High School, we were warned not to step outside the gates, but to stay on school grounds. Most high schools are surrounded by high fences and barbed wire. A government sign in front of one of the settlements reads, "Enter at your own risk." Children are taught from a young age that they must not go outside after dark for any reason because of the danger.

Local teachers explained that these townships originally were set up as temporary housing for black laborers with jobs in the cities. After apartheid ended, black South Africans flooded the camps and hoped to find good city jobs.

The terrible part about those squatters' camps is that there are lots of future young

opera singers out in those shacks as well as business people and writers and even young Nelson Mandelas who just can't make it without help. I knew I must do something to help the young people in those settlements.

I was deeply touched by the choir that had welcomed me to my Motherland when I arrived at the airport, and I wanted to thank them. When I visited Masiyile High School, I couldn't believe the conditions. Fewer than 60 teachers taught over 4,000 students; some of the handful of teachers were unqualified.

This was the high school with the most wonderful choir I ever heard and the school badly in need of a piano. So I bought a piano and taught them how to care for it. The following year, I found a South African businessman who later purchased airline tickets to the United States for them. But that wasn't enough; I wanted to do more immediately. I knew I could not help all 4,000, so I decided to start helping as many as possible.

Working with the community leaders, I founded a private high school in Claremont, a few miles from Khayelitsha Township, where the students live. The school opened in January 1997 in what had been a five-bedroom private home. Against my wishes, the school's teachers and students named it Simon Estes High School. The school is a typical high school, but with a strong emphasis on music.

Because these students come from severe poverty, the school offers hot meals, health services, and clothing. My International Foundation for Children supports the school.

We now have 150 students enrolled and plans for expanded future enrollment. Our property is large enough for a school three times as large as the current building.

The school's choir has sung for Nelson Mandela and has won many competitions in South Africa. For the 1998–99 school year, 40 members of this choir are attending schools in Iowa, living with local host families, and performing as the Simon Estes Youth Chorus. Their choir director, Nolufefe Mtshabe, is accompanying the chorus to Iowa and directing the group during their stay. Since these students have never been to the United States, I wanted an adult they knew and trusted to be with them. We were careful to enroll at least two students in each participating school so that no student would have to be completely alone. My sister Erdyne Whiteside found host families and devotes much of her time and energy to this project.

Consistent with their mission of international service and service to youth, 60 Iowa Rotary International Clubs in District 6000 have provided strong support for the choir. In addition, the project is underwritten by contributions from corporations, foundations, and individuals. In her letter, Nozipho Ngele, principal of the Simon Estes Music High School, expressed her gratitude to the many people making this experience possible.

"…We are aware of the amount of time and energy that must have been spent, to say nothing about money.

"To us, the fact that the whole 40 pupils [are] coming not only from one country but from one single school is something that will never be forgotten and it will form part of the history of the school and our lives.

"…May God Bless you all and make you go from strength to strength with your work."

This project greatly advances the education of the South African youngsters. It also expands their musical talents and intellectual potential. It offers hope to young people whose prior experiences have denied it. The project also benefits Americans who better understand the needs, interests, and culture of these and other black South Africans. It promotes peace and good will. A highlight was the opportunity for the chorus to perform for the Archbishop Desmond Tutu in the Richard Levitt Distinguished Lecture Series at the University of Iowa in Iowa City.

Although the high school is the culmination of my vision, it has required the time and

I enjoy the children's perspectives on "Porgy and Bess."

energy of many, many individuals to make it come true. The Simon Estes High School could not exist without the help of so many people. Individuals and corporations donate funds so necessary for the school to continue. They have my deep gratitude and appreciation.

Now that music and opera are open to South Africans, I am only doing my part to open doors for talented young people who would otherwise be held back by poverty. People often seem amazed at the energy and commitment it has taken to make the high school a reality. I have learned that when we are doing the right things, God provides whatever energy we need to complete the task. To me, it was just something that had to be done.

American Black
Achievement Award

PRESENTED BY
EBONY MAGAZINE
TO

Simon Estes

In recognition of your significant and enduring achievements in

Fine Arts

and for your inspiring commitment to excellence that has contributed greatly to the advancement of your fellow Black Americans and thereby enhanced the cause of brotherhood in our nation and throughout the world, the editors of Ebony Magazine have selected you to receive this award for the year 1985.

DATE

EDITOR AND PUBLISHER

My Message

A student once asked if I think we are victims of fate or makers of our own destiny. "Makers of our own destiny," I quickly answered. We are all born into a certain environment and it can be hard to overcome. So, then, how do you do it? First, every institution, whether educational or governmental or business, must have a leader. Someone needs to inspire those who are at the lowest point of their lives.

Second, we have to teach people to want something better. We have to teach them that no matter how bad the situation is, they can overcome it.

Third, we have to let the people who are in despair know that we care about them. They need examples of people who have come from those depths and succeeded.

Fourth, we need to teach them about a power greater than ourselves. That can be learned in a synagogue or church or mosque. I believe it is vitally important that people worship regularly.

What can we as a community do to facilitate young people's success? In groups as parents, religious leaders, teachers, and neighborhoods, communities need to discuss the needs of their young people and how they can help them in all phases of their lives.

We need to turn the clock back to basic values and traditions founded on trust, hard work, dedication, honesty. In the old days people shook hands and that was an unbreakable contract. In the same way they bartered with each other for goods and services, we need to come together and discuss the needs of the children and how we can barter our services and time to help them.

We all have had problems in our lives, but we still have an obligation to the children.

My life's work has been fulfilling, happy, and rewarding. I have been so incredibly blessed. My mother enjoys good health, my daughters are thriving, I have enough to eat, I can help other people, I have close and supportive friends.

As I grow older, I reflect on how I would like to be remembered.

My choice would be for people to remember me as a human being who was a servant, a messenger of God who loved and cared about others no matter where they were in the world…a person who really didn't think much about himself…a man who really loved his Creator and gained strength from Him.

When I was a child, I loved to share. I gave things away, never expecting something in return. I hope to be remembered as a man who cared, who wanted to share, and who loved.

My fondest wish is that people feel my life and my music have made a difference.

> We are looking forward to having Simon Estes return to Iowa State to work with our students, since two of our most talented graduates attend The Juilliard on scholarship through his efforts.
>
> —Janet Alcorn
> Associate
> Professor of Voice

SIMON ESTES
HONORARY DEGREE DOCTOR OF HUMANE LETTERS

Simon Estes, world renowned bass-baritone, receives the Doctor of Humane Letters for his extraordinary achievements in operatic music, philanthropy, and generosity to disadvantaged children.

Mr. Estes was born in Centerville, Iowa, and first sang at age eight in the community's Second Baptist Church. He studied with Charles Kellis, his first and only voice teacher, at the University of Iowa from 1956 to 1963. From 1964 to 1965, he studied at the Juilliard School of Music, New York City. He has been a faculty member at Juilliard since 1986.

His operatic debut was in 1965, as Ramfis in *Aida*, with the Deutsche Oper in Berlin. Since then, he has performed with all the major international opera companies. Of the nearly 90 roles in his repertoire, he most often is associated with King Philip in *Don Carlos*, Wotan in Wagner's *Ring* cycle, King Mark in *Tristan and Isolde*, Escamillo in *Carmen*, Porgy in *Porgy and Bess*, and the title roles in *Boris Godunov* and Verdi's *Attila* and *Macbeth* and *The Flying Dutchman*.

Mr. Estes also appears regularly as a recitalist and orchestral soloist with groups such as the Berlin Philharmonic, Boston Symphony, New York Philharmonic, The Philharmonia Orchestra of London and the Vienna Philharmonic.

Mr. Estes has perform at the 25th and 50th anni

In spite of all the trav time to share his knowl kindergarten through c teaches not only music

In October 1992 he during a week-long res of George Washington American student. He prior to the Homecom and musicians at a c

Mr. Estes has esta In addition, the Sim in 1993, assists une care needs. He has South African youth.

In 1996 Mr. Estes received the Iowa Awa award.

Recipients of an honorary degree from Iowa State University must have careers of superlative creative or intellectual stature. Their accomplishments must reflect the high standards of scholarship, research and/or creative ability held by Iowa State University.

— From the Spring Iowa State University Commencement program and read by Faculty Senate President William Woodman at commencement ceremonies May 10, 1997, at Hilton Coliseum, Ames, Iowa

IOWA STATE UNIVERSITY

I have received honorary degrees from Luther College, Siena College, Iowa State University, and Lawrence University, among others.

Major General Warren G. Lawson named me an Honorary Colonel in the Iowa National Guard—they even allowed me to fly an F-16 fighter jet! Of course, my military "career" pales in comparison to that of the late General Calvin Waller (my first cousin Marion Estes' husband), who served as second-in-command under General Norman Schwarzkopf in Desert Storm.

I have sung for popes, presidents, royalty, and some of the world's most recognized celebrities.

being privileged to sing for
national and international
leaders reminds me that we
are put on earth for two
reasons: to serve God and to
serve others.

VILSACK ~ PEDERSON
1999
INAUGURAL
TODAY'S DREAMS
TOMORROW'S IOWA

The Governor's Musical Gala
January 14, 1999
Master of Ceremonies
Pat Boddy
...ay's Dreams, Tomorrow's Iowa ~ Reaching for the Stars
Kaitlyn Busbee   Brooke Xaykose
Corrie Mitchell   Catalina Xaykose
                    Chayla Robinson
Simon Estes
Accompanied by Juli...

I have sung for former Iowa Governors Robert D. Ray
and Terry Branstad. Most recently I sang at the Governor's
Musical Gala featuring Ray Charles, for the inauguration of Tom
Vilsack and Lt. Governor Sally Pederson. Well-known Iowa business
and civic leaders also attended.

Ray Charles

Those of us who know Simon Estes think of him not only as a world-renowned artist, but one of the great humanitarians and teachers of what is good in America. I don't know anyone who cares more about youngsters or has a better understanding of why it is so important for the future of our great country—and the world—that children learn acceptable behavior at a very early age.

What a great influence he is in the whole world. I admire him greatly and cherish his friendship.

—Robert D. Ray,
Former Governor of Iowa

Simon Estes grew up in Centerville, Iowa, and now lives in Switzerland, but he has never forgotten his roots in Iowa. He has established several scholarship funds which benefit young people in this state. During our State's sesquicentennial year, I was very pleased to present our highest citizen award to Simon Estes in recognition of his outstanding service in the arts. He has earned a distinguished place in our history.

—Terry Branstad,
Former Governor of Iowa

In this original painting to benefit restoration of the second Baptist Church in Centerville, Iowa, where I sang as a child, the world-renowned artist P. Buckley Moss included my three daughters. Other celebrities including Cindy Crawford have donated their time and talents for worthy causes such as the golf benefit for my Foundation in Switzerland co-founded by Margarita Reich.

My sister, Erdyne, worked with key leaders from Rotary District 6000 to help bring The Simon Estes South African Youth Chorus and their director, Nolufefe Mtshabe, to Iowa to study and sing. Nolden Gentry, Chairman of Fundraising, and Committee Chair John Cortesio were both students who attended the University of Iowa with me. Nolden and I were both out for track, but when I quit to sing with the Old Gold Singers, he told me I was "wasting my time with those folks!"

EPILOGUE

My Final Concert

All careers come to an end—some sooner than we anticipate, some far into the future. When the time comes for me to leave the world of opera and singing and make way for another generation, I know what I would like to do. It would certainly be my privilege to give my final performance in Washington, D.C., this city which represents the United States of America and our government—a government of, by, and for all people.

The Kennedy Center in Washington, D.C. seems the perfect setting for staging my final concert. I was honored to sing for the opening of that prestigious concert hall in 1973, and for subsequent performances in 1996 and 1998.

Before the concert begins, I will pray just as I have before all performances throughout my career, thanking God for the gift He's given me to sing, the gift to love, the gift to care, and the gift to share. I always pray that in the audience hearts will be touched to love God and others.

As a departure from the usual concert, for my final concert I will choose both orchestral and piano accompaniment.

My program will encompass operatic arias; oratorios from Handel's *Messiah* or Haydn's *Creation;* religious songs, especially "Precious Lord, Take My Hand"; negro spirituals; and American songs such as "Without a Song" and "You'll Never Walk Alone." These selections speak of my love for God, the gift He gave me, the values my parents taught me and the person I hope I have become.

Next I would choose a conductor with the musical and spiritual qualities of a Carlo Giulini for the podium. I have found each performance with him to be a religious, musical, and artistic experience.

My final concert should reflect my work to remove barriers of economics and ethnicity, and to promote love and peace among all people. To perform with me, I would like to include a female and a male professional vocalist, and a young promising artist.

Every concert needs a finale, and mine will end with two songs: Mahler's "Ich bin der Welt Abhanden Gekommen" with a theme of "I live alone in my heaven, love, and in my song," and "The Lord is My Light," by Allitson:

> *The Lord is my Light*
> *and my salvation.*
> *Whom then shall I fear?...*
> *The Lord is the strength of my life.*

Instead of singing a traditional encore, I will call forward the young promising artist and announce to the audience, "Ladies and gentlemen, this is your encore who will carry the torch on to the future."

I will exit stage right, leaving my legacy on stage—with the spotlight focused on the next generation.

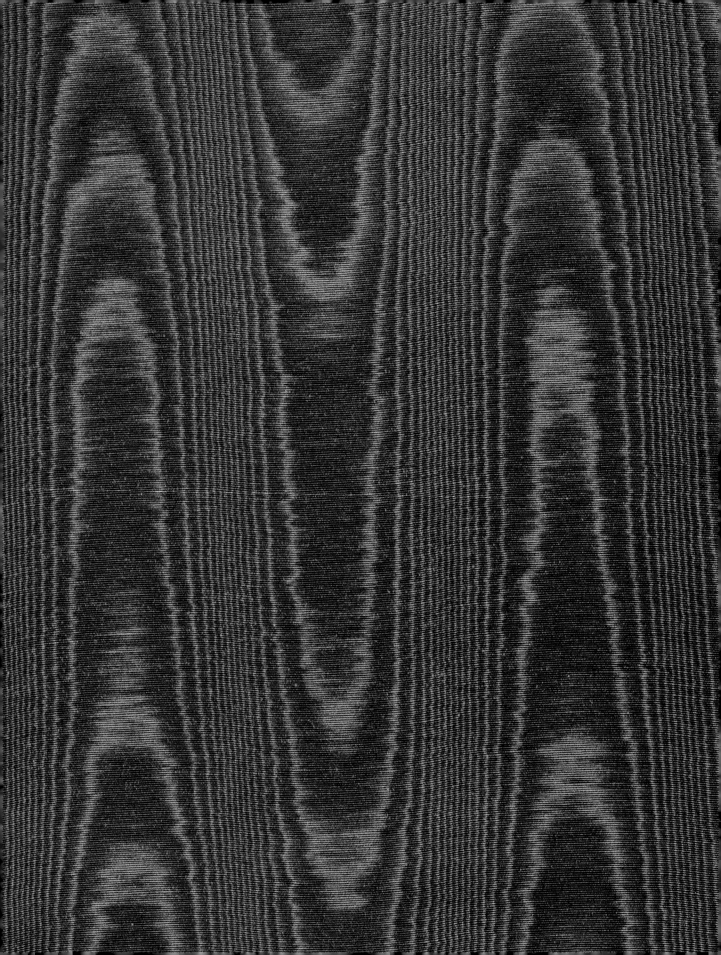

ACKNOWLEGEMENTS

From Simon Estes

I wish to thank all those who inspired me to write this book, especially my three daughters, Jennifer, Lynne, and Tiffany, whom I love more than anything.

I wish to thank my dear friend Mary Carpenter Swanson. Without her dedication and love for this story, this book would not have been written. We are both from Centerville, Iowa, from different backgrounds, who came together to write a book that we hope will be inspirational, enjoyable, and educational. You are a very dear friend who has given 110%. Mary, I thank you for your patience with a very busy opera singer. May God bless you.

There are so many people I should acknowledge who made this book possible. Many relatives and friends who have helped Simon become Simon, especially my mother and my deceased father, my sister Erdyne and my brother Dwane as well as my late sisters Patty and Westella. Thank you all!

From Mary Swanson

I dedicate this book to my son Matthew Swanson and my daughter Jody Swanson Ross the greatest editions I ever produced and whom I love dearly. You have been so patient throughout this project and are very special to me.

I wish to thank the following people for their support and encouragement during the writing of this book.

To their father Al Swanson and his ability to Interpret that red train schedule book.

A special thanks to Dr. Bill Silag for working with this novice. Bill's dedication to this project went far beyond the call of duty and exemplifies his integrity and character.

To Cindy Hoffman, a talented writer herself, who was there from the beginning.

To Enid Coulter and Sue Gould who patiently read and shared their knowledge of literature and grammar.

To the staff at Landauer Corporation especially Becky Johnston and Jeramy Landauer.

To Ruth Estes, Erdyne Whiteside, the late Westella Estes, John Cortesio, Jr., Jane Scarlet Archer, Himie Voxman, Robert McCown, Jim Galloway, Charles Kellis, Julius Tilghman, Don Gunderson, Mitzi Gibson Katz, Judith Russell, Ken Bianchi, Sandra Losh and her staff, Four Seasons Travel (Gary and his girls), Jean Nolan and Elaine Smetana (the cheering section), the Drake Public Library in Centerville, Iowa.

To Gudrun Rohrbach who helped on many a "butterfly" hunt. Without her exact records, I would still be looking for dates and places. She is a special person and I appreciate her friendship.

I thank Simon for his friendship and his faith in my ability to do this project. Thank you, Simon for sharing your beautiful family.

From the Publisher

The publisher wishes to acknowledge the following people for their contributions to the development of this book:

Janet Alcorn, Iowa State University

Ankeny, Iowa, Community Schools, Talented and Gifted Program, Dr. Linda Delbridge

Bob Beck, former publisher of Centerville *Iowegian*

Centerville High School staff and faculty

Micki Cline, Continental Hotel

Sam D'Alfonso, Canadian Opera Company

Edie Daniels

David Delbridge

Renate Dönch, Wiener Staatsoper

Kayleen Durley, music and drama director, Centerville High School

Dwane Estes

Mrs. Ruth Estes

Gloria Faust

Bill Heusinkveld and Judy Lamb, Centerville Historical Museum

Douglas M. Ireland

Charles Kellis

John Marshall, Tulsa Opera

Barbara Neumann, Hamburgische Staatsoper

Jayne Reed, Simon Estes Educational Foundation

Margarita Reich, Simon Estes International Foundation for Children

Daniel C. Robinson, Ph.D.

Gudrun Rohrbach, personal management of Simon Estes

Jim Vickery, Rotary Club of Des Moines

Erdyne Whiteside

The publisher wishes to acknowledge the following foundations for their contributions to the development of this book:

The Simon Estes Educational Foundation
130 North Greenwood, Suite P
Tulsa, OK 74120
Phone: (918) 583-0500
Fax (918) 583-0521

Iowa Arts Council Scholarship for the Arts
Iowa Arts Council
800 East Locust Street
Des Moines, IA 50319-0290
Phone: (515) 281-4100

The Simon Estes International Foundation
for Children
Postfach 234
CH-8028 Zurich, Switzerland
Phone: (41) (1) 262 33 44

The Simon and Westella Estes Scholarship Fund
Centerville High School
600 High Street
Centerville, IA 52544
Phone: (515) 856-0610

The Simon Estes Fund
The University of Iowa Foundation
Levitt Center for University Advancement
1 West Park Road, PO Box 4550
Iowa City, IA 52244-4550
Phone: (319) 335-3305

Photo Acknowlegements

Courtesy of the Bayreuth Festival:
81, 120 (bottom right)

Courtesy of the Black Diamond Yearbook,
Centerville (IA) High School: 48, 66
(middle right)

Courtesy of Bratz Studio: 26 (bottom left)

Courtesy of the Canadian Opera Company,
Michael Cooper, photographer: 126

Courtesy of Centerville High School:
57, 66 (top)

Courtesy of Columbia Artists Management, Inc.:
71, 78

Courtesy of Fleier Photography:
26 (top and bottom right)

Courtesy of Foto Marchiori: 123 (top)

Courtesy of Georg Freuler Photo-Art-Basel-
Switzerland: 33 (top right)

Courtesy of Jessica Grell: 111 (right)

Courtesy of Gordon Guy: 59

Courtesy of GrandAngle Orange: 10, 84,
125 (bottom)

© Henry Grossman: 9 (right), 138 (top right),
147 (top and bottom left),
148 (top right)

Courtesy of the Iowa National Guard:
69 (top), 145 (top and bottom)

Courtesy of kranichphoto, Berlin:
8 (fourth from left), 125 (top left)

Courtesy of Lawrence University:
144 (bottom right)

Courtesy of Luther College and Jolesch
Photography, Des Moines: 144

Courtesy of Koni Nordmann: 21, 68,
69 (middle), 125 (top right)

Courtesy of Chuck Offenburger:
4, 111 (left),138 (top and middle left,
bottom right)

© Opera National De Paris, Kleinefenn:
92 (top), 121 (top)

Courtesy of Opernhaus Zurich: 118, 119

Courtesy of Rudolf Oscar:
8 (right), 90 (left), 92 (bottom left)

Courtesy of Philips: 112, 115

Courtesy of Tony Plewik: 85, 120 (top left)

Courtesy of Carol Pratt: 1, 6, 127

Courtesy of Rich Sanders: 149

Courtesy of Susan Schimert-Ramme:
87 (top), 88 (bottom right),
123 (bottom right), 124 (top left)

Courtesy of Siena College: 9 (top left), 144
(top right)

Courtesy of the Simon Estes International
Foundation for Children:
134, 135, 150 (bottom)

Courtesy of Eduard Straub: 89, 123 (middle)

Courtesy of The Juilliard School, Jenna Soleo: 65

Courtesy of Tulsa Opera: 92 (bottom)

Courtesy of Tulsa World, Brandi Stafford,
photographer: 131

Courtesy of Tulsa World, Geoff Kreiger,
photographer: 132

Courtesy of the University of Iowa: 60, 62

Courtesy of the Vatican:
8 (bottom left), 146 (top)

Courtesy of WP Sellers: 26 (top right)

Courtesy of Weiner Staatsoper,
Österr. Bundestheatersverband: 88

Courtesy of the White House:
77, 146 (bottom)

This publication includes images from Corel
Photo Series 696000 and Series 461000 which
are protected by the copyright laws of the U.S.,
Canada, and elsewhere. Used under license.
(138)

This publication includes images from
PhotoDisc images which are protected by the
copyright laws of the U.S., Canada, and elsewhere. Used under license. (30, 72, 79, 3, 105,
110, 129)

APPENDICES

HONORARY DEGREES

1989:   Siena College
1991:   Luther College
1994:   Drake University
1994:   University of Tulsa
1997:   Iowa State University
1998:   Lawrence University

CAREER HIGHLIGHTS

1965:   April 19: Berlin Debut with Deutsche Oper

1965:   Munich Competition, third place

1965:   Audience with Pope Paul VI

1966:   Engaged by Columbia Artists Management, Inc.

1966:   Tchaikovsky Competition, third place

1966:   Command performance with President Johnson at the White House

1966:   Appeared on "The Tonight Show" with Veronica Tyler, another Tchaikovsky Competition winner

1967:   Created the role of Uncle Albert in Hamburg, Germany, at the premiere of Gunter Schuller's *The Visitation*

1968:   Performed the lead role of Carter Jones in San Francisco in Gunter Schuller's *The Visitation*

1970:   Concert to celebrate the 25th Anniversary of the United Nations

1971:   American premiere of Shostakovich's *Symphony No. 14* with Eugene Ormandy and the Philadelphia Orchestra

1971:   Grammy nomination for Album of the Year and Best Classical Vocal Soloist Performance for Shostakovich: *Symphony No. 14*

1972:   Olympic Games Opening Ceremonies in Munich, Germany

1973:   Opened the Concert Hall at the Kennedy Center with violinist Isaac Stern

1978:   First performance at the Bayreuth Festival in the title role of *The Flying Dutchman*

1979:   Performed the title role in *Oberto* in Bologna

1979:   Played Pharaoh in the historic revival of Rossini's *Moses* at La Scala

1981:   April 12: Metropolitan Opera, New York City, debut singing the third act of Wagner's *Die Walküre* in concert version with Birgit Nilsson

1981:   90th Anniversary of Carnegie Hall

1982:   Opened at the Metropolitan Opera singing Landgraf in Wagner's *Tannhäuser*

1982:   Bayreuth Festival, sang the role of Amfortas in a new production of *Parsifal*

1982:   Centerville, Iowa—first home-town concert as a professional singer

1983:   Sang Rossini's *Stabat Mater* at the Salzburg Festival, Austria

1984:   Academy of Vocal Arts Award for Outstanding American Singers

1984:   Leontyne Price's farewell performance at the Metropolitan Opera, *Aida*

1985:   Played Porgy at the Metropolitan Opera premiere of *Porgy and Bess*

1985:   Solo Wagner album won France's Grand Prix du Disque for operatic solo album

1985:   Became a professor at The Juilliard School of Music

1986:   July 4: Statue of Liberty Centennial Celebration, New York City, with the Boston Pops Orchestra

1986:   Opened the Met season as Wotan in *Die Walküre*

1989:   "In Performance at the White House" (televised) with President George Bush

1990:   Performed at the Inauguration Ceremony for Governor Wilder of Virginia, the first black United States governor,

1990:   Performance at a White House State Dinner honoring Corazón Aquino

1990:   Performance at Riverside Baptist Church for Nelson Mandela

1990: Independence Day Celebration performance at the Washington, DC Mall with the National Symphony Orchestra, Mstislav Rostropovich conducting

1990: Soloist at "The Anatomy of Hate" conference in Oslo, Norway for the Nobel Peace Prize Committee and the Elie Wiesel Foundation for Humanity

1990: Berlin Concert recognizing the re-unification of Germany

1991: Audience with Pope John Paul II

1991: Performed the title role in the London premier of King

1992: Performed at an Independence Day celebration for the US Ambassador to Switzerland at the Embassy in Berne

1993: Concert at Gewandhaus Leipzig, Germany, to celebrate 250th Anniversary of the Gewandhaus Orchestra with Kurt Masur conducting

1993: Performed the title role in a new production of Boris Godunov at the Leipzig, Germany Opera House's 300th Anniversary Celebration

1993: Luncheon for Congressional Wives with Hillary Clinton

1993: Bamberg, inauguration of the new concert hall with Mahler's Symphony No. 8

1994: Performed for Archbishop Desmond Tutu in the Cathedral of St. John the Divine, New York City

1994: Simon Estes Auditorium dedicated in Centerville, Iowa

1994: Opening of the Berliner Festwochen as Count Cenci in the German premiere of Berthold Goldschmidt's opera Beatrice Cenci in presence of the composer

1994: Gala Performance for the opening of The New Isreali Opera House, Tel Aviv, Isreal

1995: Cape Town, South Africa role debut in the title role of Nabucco

1995: Concert to celebrate the 50th anniversary of the United Nations, New York City

1996: Sang the title role in Porgy and Bess in Cape Town, South Africa

1996: Good Friday Performance for Archbishop Desmond Tutu, St. George Cathedral, Cape Town, South Africa

1996: Presented with the Iowa Award by Governor Terry Branstad

1996: Simon Estes Ampitheatre dedicated, Des Moines, Iowa

1996: 50th Anniversary of Iowa All-State Music Festival

1997: Performed title role in King for the Presidential Inauguration Ceremonies

1997: The Simon Estes High School founded in Cape Town, South Africa

1997: Named a Paul Harris Fellow of Rotary International

1997-98: Iowa Concert Tour

1998: Sang at the ceremony for the 50th Anniversary of the Berlin Airlift

1998: Kennedy Center title role debut in Simon Boccanegra with Placido Domingo

PERFORMANCES FOR WORLD LEADERS

William Clinton, President of the United States
George Bush, President of the United States
Jimmy Carter, President of the United States
Lyndon Johnson, President of the United States
Richard Nixon, President of the United States
Byron Mulroney, Prime Minister of Canada
Vaclav Havel, President of Czechoslovakia
François Mitterand, President of France
Helmut Kohl, Federal Chancellor of Federal Republic of Germany and re-united Germany
Helmut Schmidt, Federal Chancellor of Federal Republic of Germany
Richard von Weizsâcker, Federal President of Federal Republic of Germany
Yassar Arafat, Palestine Liberation Organization Chairman and Palestine National Authority President
Yitzhak Rabin, Prime Minister of Israel
Shimon Peres, Prime Minister of Israel
Boris Yeltsin, President of Russia
Nelson Mandela, President of South Africa
Prince Rainier III of Monaco
King Harald and Queen Sonja of Norway
King Olaf V of Norway
King Juan Carlos of Spain
Corazón Aquino, President of the Philippines

DISCOGRAPHY

Beethoven: Symphonie no 9
    conductor: Giulini
    Varady, van Nes, Lewis, Estes
    PGDI/Deutsche Grammaphon

Berlioz: Romeo et Juliette; Les Nuits d'Eté
    conductor: Muti; Barbirolli
    Norman, Aler, Estes
    Philadelphia Orchestra;
    New Philharmonia Orchestra
    EMD/EMI Classics

Bizet: Carmen
    conductor: Ozawa
    Norman, Freni, Schicoff, Estes
    ORTF National Orchestra,
    French National Radio Chorus
    Philips
    (also available as Highlights)

Classic Aid Gala 1988
    conductor: Maazel
    Domingo, Estes, Hendricks,
    Orchestre National de France
    Philips

De Falla: Atlantida
    conductor: Colomer
    Estes, Bayo, Berganza
    Joven Orquesta Nacional de Espana,
    Auvidis-Valois

DeMars: An American Requiem
    conductor: DeMars
    Estes, Childs, Breault, Luna,
    The Mormon Tabernacle Choir
    BWE

Fauré: Requiem Op. 48
    conductor: Davis
    Popp, Estes
    Radio Chorus Leipzig,
    Dresden State Orchestra
    Philips

From Opera to Gospel
    Estes
    Praise Productions

Gershwin: Porgy and Bess Highlights
    conductor: Slatkin
    Estes, Alexander
    Berlin Radio Chorus,
    Berlin Radio Symphony
    Philips

Goldschmidt: Beatrice Cenci; Lieder
    conductor: Zagrosek
    Alexander, Estes, Jones, Kimm
    Deutsches Symphonie-Orchestra Berlin
    Sony

Haydn: Leonard Bernstein: The Royal Edition,
    vol. 36 and 37
    conductor: Bernstein
    Sony

International Tchaikovsky Competition, vol. 3:
    Great Vocalists
    Marsh, Atlantov, Estes, Obraztsova
    BMG/Melodiya

Mahler: Symphony no 8
    conductor: Gielen
    Robinson, Marshall, Heichele, Wenkel, Estes
    Sony

Mozart: Idomeneo
    conductor: Harnoncourt
    Hollweg, Schmidt, Yakar, Estes
    Teldec
    (also available as Highlights)

Mozart: Requiem
    conductor: Giulini
    Dawson, van Nes, Lewis, Estes
    Philharmonia Orchestra
    Sony

Ol' Man River: Broadway's Greatest Hits
    conductor: Waters
    Estes
    Munich Radio Orchestra,
    Bavarian Radio Chorus
    Philips

Saint-Saëns: Samson et Dalila
    conductor: Davis
    Baltsa, Carreras, Summers, Estes, Burchuladze
    Philips
    (also available as Highlights)

Spirituals
    Estes
    Philips

Steal Away: My Favorite Negro Spirituals
    Estes
    Ryan, Piano
    Deutsche Schallplatten

Stravinsky: L'Histoire du Soldat
    conductor: Dutoit
    Estes, Berthet, Carrat, Simon
    Teldec

Stravinsky: Oedipus Rex
    conductor: Salonen
    Cole, vonOtter, Estes, Soltin, Gedda
    Swedish Radio Symphony Orchestra,
    Eric Ericson Chamber Choir
    Sony

Stravinsky: Pulcinella
    conductor: Boulez
    Murray, Estes, Rolfe-Johnson
    Teldec

Verdi: Don Carlos
    conductor: Giulini
    Domingo, Caballé, Raimondi, Estes,
    Orchestra of the Royal Opera House,
    Covent Garden
    EMI Classics

Verdi: Oberto
    Fonit Cetra Italia/Musica Aperta
    conductor: Peskó
    Cortez, Grilli, Estes, Grulin
    Teatro Comunale di Bologna Orchestra, Choir

Verdi: Arias
    conductor: Delogu
    Estes
    New Philharmonica Orchestra
    Philips

Verdi: Requiem
    conductor: Schneidt
    Sweet, van Nes, Araiza, Estes
    BMG/Arte Nova

Wagner: The Flying Dutchman
    conductor: Nelsson
    Estes, Balslev, Salminen, Schunk
    Philips
    (also available as Highlights)

Wagner: Parsifal
    conductor: Levine
    Hofmann, Sotin, Estes, Mazura, Salminen
    Bayreuth Chorus and Orchestra
    Philips
    (also available as Highlights)

Wagner: Parsifal, Richard Wagner Edition
    conductor: Levine
    Hofmann, Sotin, Estes, Mazura, Salminen
    Bayreuth Chorus and Orchestra
    Philips
    (also available as Highlights)

Wagner: Arias
    Conductor: Fricke
    Estes
    Staatskatelle Berlin
    Philips

Welcome to Broadway
    Estes
    Praise Productions

SELECTED OPERA AND CONCERT PERFORMANCES

1965
Berlin, Deutsche Oper — *Aida*, Ramfis
Munich — Munich Competition

1966
Moscow — Tchaikovsky Competition

1967
Hamburg, State Opera — *The Visitation*, Uncle Albert

1968
San Francisco — *The Visitation*, Carter Jones

1969
Chicago, Lyric Opera — *Macbeth*, Banco

1971
Philadelphia — Shostakovich: *Symphony No. 14*

1976
Zurich, Opera House — *Porgy and Bess*, Porgy;
          The Flying Dutchman, Dutchman

1978
Hamburg, State Opera — *Don Carlo*, King Philip
Bayreuth, Festival — *The Flying Dutchman*, Dutchman

1979
Hamburg, State Opera —*The Flying Dutchman*,
          Dutchman
Bayreuth, Festival — *The Flying Dutchman*, Dutchman

1980
Hamburg, State Opera — *Carmen*, Escamillo
Bayreuth, Festival — *The Flying Dutchman*, Dutchman
Zurich, Opera House — *Attila*, Attila

1981
Hamburg, State Opera — *Aida*, Amonasro; *Don Carlo*,
          King Philip; *The Flying Dutchman*, Dutchman;
          Tales of Hoffmann, Lindorf, Coppelius,
          Dapertutto, Dr. Miracle
Bayreuth, Festival — *The Flying Dutchman*, Dutchman

1982
Bayreuth, Festival — *Parsifal*, Amfortas;
          The Flying Dutchman, Dutchman

Berlin, Deutsche Oper — *Aida*, Amonasro;
          The Flying Dutchman, Dutchman
Philadelphia, PA — *Roméo et Juilette*
Zurich, Opera House — *Saul*, Saul
Hamburg, Musikhalle — Beethoven: *Symphony No. 9*
New York, NY, Metropolitan Opera — *Tannhäuser*, Landgraf
Recital: Chicago, IL

1983
Zurich, Opera House — *Saul*, Saul
Geneva, Grand Théâtre — *Salome*, Jochanaan
Zurich, Hallenstadion — *Aida*, Amonasro
Bayreuth, Festival — *Parsifal*, Amfortas
Salzburg, Festival — Rossini: *Stabat Mater*
Philadelphia, PA — *Macbeth*, Banco
New York, NY, Carnegie Hall — *Macbeth*, Banco
Barcelona, Gran Teatro del Liceo — *The Flying Dutchman*,
          Dutchman; *Aida*, Amonasro

1984
Chicago, IL — Beethoven: *Missa Solemnis*
Washington, DC — Beethoven: *Missa Solemnis*
Houston, TX — Berlioz: *Damnation of Faust*
New York, NY — Haydn: *The Creation*
New York Metropolitan Opera Tour — *Die Walküre*,
          Wotan; Washington, DC; Atlanta, GA; Dallas,
          TX; Minneapolis, MN; Detroit, MI; Toronto,
          ON; Cleveland, OH
Orange, Chorégies — *Don Carlo*, King Philip
Bayreuth, Festival — *The Flying Dutchman*, Dutchman;
          Parsifal, Amfortas
Berlin, Deutsche Oper — *Aida*, Amonasro;
          Das Rheingold, Wotan; *Die Walküre*, Wotan
Munich, Herkulessaal — Handel: *Messiah*
New York, NY, Metropolitan Opera — *Elektra*,
          Orestes; *Aida*, Amonasro
Paris, Salle Pleyel — *Die Walküre*, Wotan, concert version
Recitals: New York, Carnegie Hall; Frankfurt,
          Alte Oper; Berlin, Deutsche Oper
Concert: Des Moines, IA

1985
New York, NY, Metropolitan Opera — *Aida*,
          Amonasro; *Porgy and Bess*, Porgy; *Parsifal*,
          Amfortas; Florence, Maggio Musicale —
          Don Carlo, King Philip

Bayreuth, Festival — *Parsifal*, Amfortas;
    The Flying Dutchman, Dutchman
Zurich, Opera House — *Macbeth*, Macbeth
Berlin, Deutsche Oper — *Das Rheingold*, Wotan;
    Die Walküre, Wotan
Munich, State Opera — *Macbeth*, Macbeth
Recital: Paris, Théâtre des Champs-Elysées

1986
Zurich, Opera House — *Salome*, Jochanaan;
    Macbeth, Macbeth
London, Covent Garden — *The Flying Dutchman*,
    Dutchman
New York, NY, Metropolitan Opera — *Parsifal*,
    Amfortas; *Die Walküre*, Wotan
Tulsa, OK, Opera — *Porgy and Bess*, Porgy
Concert: New York City, NY, Statue of Liberty
    Centennial Celebration

1987
New York, NY, Avery Fisher Hall — Shostakovich:
    Symphony No. 14
New York, NY, Metropolitan Opera — *Die Walküre*,
    Wotan; *Parsifal*, Amfortas
Berlin, Deutsche Oper — *The Flying Dutchman*,
    Dutchman
Zurich, Opera House — *Aida*, Amonasro
Orange, Chorégies — *The Flying Dutchman*, Dutchman
Frankfurt, Alte Oper — Verdi: *Requiem*
Hamburg, State Opera — *The Flying Dutchman,*
    Dutchman
Paris, Palais Garnier — *Macbeth*, Macbeth
Recitals: New York, NY, Metropolitan Museum of Art;
    New York, NY, Carnegie Hall; Toronto, Roy
    Thomson Hall; Lucerne, International Festival

1988
Frankfurt, Opera House — *The Flying Dutchman,*
    Dutchman
London, Covent Garden — *Parsifal*, Amfortas
Vienna, State Opera — *The Flying Dutchman*, Dutchman;
    Die Walküre, Wotan; *Macbeth*, Macbeth
Berlin, Deutsche Oper — *Das Rheingold*, Wotan;
    Die Walküre, Wotan; *The Flying Dutchman*,
    Dutchman
Orange, Chorégies — *Das Rheingold*, Wotan
Brussels, Palais des Beaux Arts — Beethoven:
    Symphony No. 9
Madrid, Auditorio Nacional Musica — Verdi: *Requiem*
Munich, Philharmonie — Verdi: *Requiem*

Milan, Cathedral — Verdi: *Requiem*
Barcelona, Gran Teatro del Liceo — *Parsifal*, Amfortas
Chicago, IL, Orchestra Hall — *Simon Boccanegra*,
    Fiesco, concert version

1989
Berlin, Deutsche Oper — *Flying Dutchman*, Dutchman;
    Aida, Amonasro
Paris, Chatelet — Mahler: *Symphony No. 8*
London, Royal Festival Hall — Mozart: *Requiem*
Frankfurt, Opera House — *Flying Dutchman*, Dutchman
Toronto, Roy Thomson Hall — Verdi: *Requiem*
Montreal, Notre-Dame Basilica — Verdi: *Requiem*
Ottawa, National Arts Centre — Verdi: *Requiem*
Zurich, Tonhalle — Brahms: *Four Serious Songs*
Vienna, State Opera — *Aida*, Amonasro
Recitals — Bonn, Opera House; Paris, Chatelet;
    Berlin, Deutsche Oper

1990
Hamburg, State Opera — *Flying Dutchman*, Dutchman
London, England — *King*, King
Bonn, Opera House — *Macbeth*, Macbeth; *Das Rheingold*,
    Wotan
Stuttgart, Opera House — *Flying Dutchman*, Dutchman
Zurich, Tonhalle — Beethoven: *Symphony No. 9*
Berlin, Deutsche Oper — *Salome*, Jochanaan; *Flying
    Dutchman*, Dutchman
New York, NY — Beethoven: *Symphony No. 9*
Bonn, Beethovenhalle — Verdi: *Requiem*
Cologne, Philharmonie — Verdi: *Requiem*
Barcelona, Gran Teatro del Liceo — *Die Walküre*, Wotan
Concerts: Washington, DC, Capitol, National
    Symphony Orchestra with Mstislav
    Rostropovich; Oslo, Conference on "The
    Anatomy of Hate"

1991
Berlin, Deutsche Oper — *Aida*, Amonasro; *Flying
    Dutchman*, Dutchman
Zurich, Opera House — *Elektra*, Orestes; *La Forza del
    Destino*, Padre Guardiano
Olso, Concert Hall — Verdi: *Requiem*
Philadelphia, PA — Brahms: *Requiem*; Academy of Music,
    Mozart: *Requiem*
Vienna, State Opera — *Die Walküre*, Wotan
Munich, State Opera — *Parsifal*, Amfortas;
    The Flying Dutchman, Dutchman
Stockholm, Berwald Hall — *Oedipus Rex*,
    Kreon, Messenger

Washington, DC, Kennedy Center — Beethoven: *Symphony No. 9*

New York City, NY — Beethoven: *Symphony No. 9*; Mozart: *Requiem*

Festival de St. Denis, Basilica — *Mosé*, Mosé

Berlin, Konische Oper — Verdi: *Requiem*

Orange, Chorégies — *Elektra*, Orestes; *Aida*, Amonasro

Ravinia, Il — Handel: *Messiah*

Barcelona, Gran Teatro del Liceo — *Salome*, Jochanaan

Rome, Sala Nervi, Vatican — Mozart: *Requiem*

Recitals: Munich, Herkulessaal; Las Palmas de Gran Canaria; Santa Cruz de Tenerife; Frankfurt, Alte Oper; Berlin, Deutsche Oper; Santander, Festival; Bonn, Opera House

Concerts: Festival de Peralada; Des Moines, IA, Civic Center; Ames, IA; Valencia, Palau de la Musica

1992

Zurich, Opera House — *La Forza del Destino*, Padre Guardiano; *Carmen*, Escamillo

Berlin, Deutsche Oper — *Aida*, Amonasro; *The Flying Dutchman*, Dutchman; *La Forza del Destino*, Padre Guardiano

Zurich, Tonhalle — Haydn: *The Creation*

Las Palmas de Gran Canaria — *Don Carlo*, King Philip

Leipzig, Opera House — *The Flying Dutchman*, Dutchman

Miami, Fl, Grand Opera — *Macbeth*, Macbeth

Vienna, Musikverein — *Mosé*, Mosé

Bonn, Opera House — *Die Walküre*, Wotan

Berlin, Philharmonie — Verdi: *Requiem*

Santander, Palacio de Festivales — *Atlantida*, Coryphée

Sevilla, Teatro de la Maestranza — *Atlantida*, Coryphée

Valencia, Palau de la Musica — *Atlantida*, Coryphée; Haydn: *The Creation*

Madrid, Auditorio Nacional — *Atlantida*, Coryphée

Hamburg, State Opera — *Die Walküre*, Wotan

Recitals: Barcelona, Gran Teatro del Liceo; New York, NY; The Juilliard School of Music

Concerts: Berlin, Komische Oper; Stockholm, Royal Opera; Prague, Prague Autumn Festival

1993

Zurich, Opera House — *Carmen*, Escamillo; *Elektra*, Orestes; *Macbeth*, Macbeth; *Don Carlo*; King Philip

Hamburg, State Opera — *Die Walküre*, Wotan

Berlin, Deutsche Oper — *The Flying Dutchman*, Dutchman; *Aida*, Amonasro; *Carmen*, Escamillo

Munich, State Opera — *Parsifal*, Amfortas

Leipzig, Opera House — *Boris Godunov*, Boris

Lyon, Auditorium Maurice Ravel — Mahler: *Symphony No. 8*

Berlin, Philharmonie — Brahms: *Requiem*

Madrid, Teatro Nacional Zarzuela — *The Flying Dutchman*, Dutchman

Peralada, Festival — *The Flying Dutchman*, Dutchman

Bamberg, Concert Hall — Mahler: *Symphony No. 8*

Paris, Opéra Bastille — *The Flying Dutchman*, Dutchman

Cleveland, OH, Severance Hall — Fauré: *Requiem*

Zurich, Hallenstadion — *Carmen*, Escamillo

Recitals: Munich, Herkulessaal; Valencia, Palau de la Musica; Torino, Conservatorio G. Verdi; Catania, Teatro Bellini

Concerts: Leipzig, Gewandhaus; Bamberg, Concert Hall

1994

Berlin, Deutsche Oper — *The Flying Dutchman*, Dutchman; *Macbeth*, Macbeth; *Carmen*, Escamillo; *Don Carlo*, King Philip

Hamburg, State Opera — *Die Walküre*, Wotan

Bordeaux, Grand Théâtre — Haydn: *The Creation*

Valencia, Palau de la Musica — Verdi: *Requiem*

Vienna, State Opera — *Salome*, Jochanaan

Orange, Chorégies — *Nabucco*, Zaccaria

Berlin, Philharmonie — *Beatrice Cenci*, Cenci

Lisbon — Mahler: *Symphony No. 8*

Barcelona, Palau de la Musica — Haydn: *The Creation*

Recitals: Zurich, Tonhalle; Centerville, IA; Ludwigsburg, Festival

Concerts: Tel-Aviv, New Israeli Opera House; Madrid, Teatro de la Zarzuela, *Tristan and Isolde*, King Mark; Santa Cruz de Tenerife, Teatro; Zurich, Tonhalle, Benefit for The Simon Estes International Foundation for Children

1995

Zurich, Opera House — *Carmen*, Escamillo; *The Flying Dutchman*, Dutchman; *La Forza del Destino*, Padre Guardiano

Nice, Opéra — *The Flying Dutchman*, Dutchman

Berlin, Deutsche Oper — *Aida*, Amonasro; *The Flying Dutchman*, Dutchman

Cape Town, Nico Opera House — *Nabucco*, Nabucco

Vilnius, Philharmonic Hall — Verdi: *Requiem*

Hamburg, State Opera — *Die Walküre*, Wotan

Monte-Carlo, Palais Princier de Monaco — Verdi: *Requiem*

Washington, DC, Kennedy Center — DeMars: *An American Requiem*

New York City, NY, St. John the Divine — DeMars:
  An American Requiem
Linz, International Bruckner Festival — *Die Walküre*, Wotan
London, Covent Garden — *Aida*, Amonasro
Cape Town, Nico Opera House — *Nabucco*, Nabucco
Recitals: Berlin, Deutsche Oper; Hamburg, State
  Opera; Bamburg, Concert Hall; Bonn, Opera
  House; Ossiach, Festival Carinthischer
Concerts: Munich, Philharmonie;
  Bordeaux, Grand Théâtre; Des Moines, IA,
  Civic Center; Linz, Landestheater; Munich,
  Philharmonie; Bern, Casino; Basel, Stadtcasino

1996

Berlin, Deutsche Oper — *Aida*, Amonasro
Zurich, Opera House — *Carmen*, Escamillo; *The Flying
  Dutchman*, Dutchman
Cape Town, Nico Opera House — *Porgy and Bess*, Porgy
London, Covent Garden — *Nabucco*, Zaccaria
Bordeaux — Mahler: *Symphony No. 8*
Brooklyn, NY, Academy of Music — Beethoven:
  Symphony No. 9
New York City, NY, Avery Fisher Hall — Beethoven:
  Symphony No. 9
Hamburg, State Opera— *Carmen*, Escamillo
Toronto, ON, Canadian Opera — *Salome*, Jochanaan
Cape Town, Nico Opera House — *Porgy and Bess*, Porgy
Salt Lake City, UT, Salt Lake Tabernacle — DeMars:
  An American Requiem
Hamburg, Michalis Church — Beethoven: *Missa Solemnis*
Bordeaux, Grand Théâtre — *Tosca*, Scarpia, concert version
Santa Cruz de Tenerife — *Die Walküre*, Wotan,
  concert version
Recitals: Washington, DC, Kennedy Center; Fort
  Dodge, IA; Zurich, Opera House; Gowrie, IA;
  San Juan, Festical Casals; Ossiach, Festival
  Carinthischer Sommer; Nevada, IA; Baltimore,
  MD, Meyerhoff Symphony Hall; Ames, IA,
  Iowa State University; Munich, Herkulessaal
Concerts: Bregenz, Festspielhaus; Lucerne, Kunsthaus;
  Lille, Nouveau Siécle; Paris, Théâtre des
  Champs Elysées; Zurich, Tonhalle; Des
  Moines, IA, Civic Center; Durban, City Hall;
  Cape Town, Nico Opera House; Vienna,
  Musikverein; Graz, Opera House;
  Munich, Prinzregenztheater

1997

Zurich, Opera House — *The Flying Dutchman*,
  Dutchman; *Carmen*, Escamillo

Washington, DC, Mall — Inauguration Festivities
Berlin, Deutsche Oper — *Aida*, Amonasro; *Tosca*,
  Scarpia; *Das Rheingold*, Wotan; *Siegfried*,
  Wanderer
Hamburg, State Opera — *Die Walküre*, Wotan;
  The Flying Dutchman, Dutchman
Vienna, State Opera — *Carmen*, Escamillo;
  Aida, Amonasro
Hamburg, Michaelis Church — Brahms: *Requiem*
Munich, State Opera — *The Flying Dutchman*, Dutchman
Perlada, Festival — *The Flying Dutchman*, Dutchman
Recitals: San Juan, Festival Casals; Peralada, Festival
Concerts: Barcelona, Palau de la Musica; Des Moines,
  IA, First Federated Church; Pittsburg, PA,
  Heinz Hall; San Juan, Festival Casals; Villach,
  Festival Carinthischer Sommer; Lille, Salle
  Vauban-Grand Palais; Paris, Théâtre des
  Champs-Elysées; Canterbury, Cathedral;
  Zurich, Tonhalle; Iowa Tour

1998

Hamburg, State Opera — *Carmen*, Escamillo;
  Die Walküre, Wotan
Berlin, Deutsche Oper — *Aida*, Amonasro
Rome, Santa Cecilia — Beethoven: *Symphony No. 9*
Peralada, Festival — *Magic Flute*, Sarastro
Madrid, Teatro Real — *Aida*, Amonasro
Washington, DC, Opera — *Simon Boccanegra*, Simon
New York City, NY, Carnegie Hall — *Nabucco*, Zaccaria,
  concert version
San Juan, Festival Casals — *Nabucco*, Zaccaria,
  concert version
Cracow, Beethoven Easter Festival — *Fidelio*, Don
  Pizarro, concert version
Recitals: Mason City, IA; Okoboji, IA; Hamburg,
  Alte Post; Figueres; Carroll, IA; Ossiach,
  Festival Carinthischer Sommer; Iowa City, IA,
  Hancher Auditorium;
Concerts: Durban, City Hall; Fort Dodge, IA;
  Wiesbaden, International May Festival, The
  Three Basses; Des Moines, IA, Iowa Summit;
  Berlin Gerdarmenmarkt, Freedom Concert;
  Des Moines, IA, First Federated Church;
  Peralada, Festival; The Hague, Dr. Anton
  Philipszaal; Keowscht, Festival Zeeuwsch-
  Vlaanderen; Des Moines, IA, Des Moines
  Christian School; Zurich, Neumünster
  Church; Wettingen, Church St. Anton;
  Leuggern, St. Peter and Paul Church;
  Tulsa, OK, First Presbyterian Church